MW00955074

INDIANA TEST PREP
ILEARN Practice Test Book
English Language Arts
Grade 3

© 2018 by I. Hawas

All rights reserved. No part of this book may be reproduced or transmitted in any form or by any means, electronic, mechanical, photocopying, recording, or otherwise without prior written permission.

ISBN 978-1728723006

TEST MASTER PRESS

www.testmasterpress.com

CONTENTS

Introduction   **4**

English Language Arts Practice Sets   **5**

Set 1   Reading: Literature Text   5

Set 2   Reading: Literature Text   12

Set 3   Reading and Writing: Nonfiction Text with Persuasive Writing Task   19

Set 4   Reading and Writing: Nonfiction Text with Informative Writing Task   29

Set 5   Reading and Writing: Literature Text with Narrative Writing Task   38

Set 6   Reading: Literature Text   46

Set 7   Reading: Literature Text   52

Set 8   Reading and Writing: Nonfiction Text with Informative Writing Task   58

Set 9   Reading and Writing: Nonfiction Text with Persuasive Writing Task   66

Set 10   Reading and Writing: Literature Text with Narrative Writing Task   73

Set 11   Writing: Research, Writing Process, and Writing Conventions   81

Set 12   Reading: Nonfiction Text   90

Set 13   Reading: Literature Text   97

Set 14   Reading and Writing: Nonfiction Text with Persuasive Writing Task   104

Set 15   Reading and Writing: Nonfiction Text with Informative Writing Task   113

Set 16   Reading and Writing: Literature Text with Narrative Writing Task   122

Set 17   Reading: Nonfiction Text   130

Set 18   Reading and Writing: Paired Literature Texts with Writing Task   138

Set 19   Writing: Research, Writing Process, and Writing Conventions   146

Set 20   Reading and Writing: Paired Nonfiction Texts with Writing Task   155

Set 21   Research and Writing: Persuasive Writing Task   164

Set 22   Research and Writing: Informative Writing Task   171

Extras   **180**

Answer Key   180

Writing Rubrics   204

INTRODUCTION
For Parents, Teachers, and Tutors

About the ILEARN English/Language Arts Assessments

Beginning in the 2018-2019 school year, students in Indiana will take the new ILEARN assessments. The tests are taken online and cover reading, writing, research, vocabulary, and writing conventions. This practice book will prepare students for all the types of tasks found on the assessments.

Skills Assessed on the ILEARN English/Language Arts Assessments

The ILEARN ELA tests assess the skills listed in the Indiana Academic Standards. The reading skills assessed include reading literature texts, reading nonfiction texts, and vocabulary. The writing skills assessed include writing process, research process, and writing conventions. This book includes sets that focus on each of the areas tested and covers all the skills assessed on the test.

Types of Questions on the ILEARN English/Language Arts Assessments

The ILEARN tests are taken online and include a wide range of question types, including technology-enhanced items. These question types are described below.

- Multiple Choice – students select the one correct answer from four possible options.
- Multiple Select – students select all the correct answers from the possible options.
- Evidence-Based Selected Response – students answer a question about a passage, and then answer a related question that asks students to select evidence that supports their answer.
- Short Answer – students provide a short written answer.
- Hot text – students select words, phrases, or sentences to answer a question.
- Graphic Response – students complete a web or diagram.
- Drag and Drop – students drag items such as words, phrases, and sentences to another location. This could involve tasks like placing items in order or adding items to a table.
- Edit Task – students replace words or phrases in a passage, either by selecting the correct option from a set of choices or by writing the correct word or phrase.
- Table Matching – students click boxes in a table to select answers.
- Writing Prompt – students write a complete essay, narrative, or opinion piece.
- Performance Task – students complete a set of research and writing tasks based on several passages, and also complete a writing task.

This book includes practice with all the question types on the test, including questions that mimic the technology-enhanced questions. It also provides practice with all the types of writing prompts.

Completing the Practice Sets

The exercises in this book are divided into convenient practice sets that increase in difficulty throughout the book. This design allows for progress to be reviewed after each set, which will help students develop and build their skills as they practice. By completing all the practice sets, students will develop all the skills they need and become familiar with all the tasks they will encounter on the real state assessments.

English Language Arts

Practice Set 1

Reading

Literature Text

Instructions

This set has one passage for you to read. The passage is followed by questions.

Read each question carefully. For each multiple-choice question, fill in the circle for the correct answer. For other types of questions, follow the instructions given. Some of the questions require a written answer. Write your answer on the lines provided.

Sarah and Janet

Sarah and her sister Janet were always competing with each other. Sarah always wanted to outdo Janet. Janet always wanted to outdo Sarah.

They liked most of the same things and this often led to fights. If Janet sang a song, Sarah wanted to sing it louder and better. If Sarah learned a new song on the piano, Janet had to learn it too and she would try to perform it better. They both wanted to be the fastest runner and the best volleyball player. They would even compete over who could finish reading a book the fastest. It drove their mother crazy.

"Why can't you girls just get along?" she would ask them time and time again. "I am so tired of hearing your bickering."

They would just shrug and keep on arguing. One day, their mother had an idea to help them get along. She planned to take them shopping at the local mall. The girls were excited about taking a shopping trip.

"Now you can both pick out something," said their mother as she parked the car outside the mall. "But choose carefully because you can each only have one outfit."

When they arrived at the mall, they entered a clothing shop. Soon enough, the girls began fighting over the clothing.

"I want this dress," Sarah stated.

"No, I want that dress," Janet said.

"I'm having it because it'll look better on me," Sarah said.

"It will not! It will look better on me," Janet said.

"Alright," said their mother quietly. "Since you both like the dress so much, you can both have one. But do you want to each pick a different color?"

"I want the blue one," Sarah quickly stated.

"No, you should get the yellow one. It would look so nice on you," Janet replied.

"You just want me to get the yellow one because you want the blue one," Sarah argued. "But I'm not being fooled. I'm getting the blue one and you can choose whatever one you want."

"Fine. Then I'm getting the blue one too."

Their mother sighed and took the two blue dresses up to the counter. She handed both Sarah and Janet their new dress and they all left the store.

The girls looked at each other. They were both confused. Usually their mother would buy them different clothes. She had never bought them the same thing before. They were happy to get what they wanted, but they returned home unsure as to what was happening.

It all became clear the following day. The girls dressed for school in their own rooms and headed downstairs for breakfast. They were shocked to see that they were both wearing the same outfit. They began to argue about who should go and change their clothes.

"Nobody is going to change their clothes," said their mother. "You both chose these clothes, so you can both wear them. Now you can see what your silly arguments have led to."

The girls giggled as they realized what their mother was saying.

1   What does the word <u>bickering</u> mean in the sentence below?

        "I am so tired of hearing your bickering."

     Ⓐ   Fighting

     Ⓑ   Complaining

     Ⓒ   Singing

     Ⓓ   Competing

2   Which meaning of the word <u>clear</u> is used in the sentence below?

        It all became clear the following day.

     Ⓐ   Able to be seen through

     Ⓑ   Fine or nice

     Ⓒ   Understood or known

     Ⓓ   Sounding pleasant

3   Complete the web with **three** more examples of Sarah and Janet competing with each other.

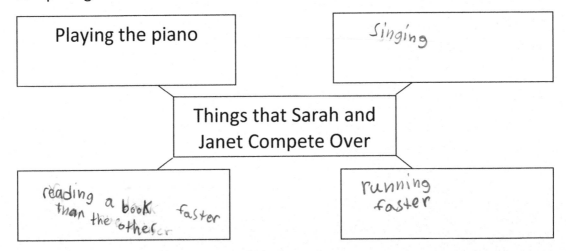

4   What is the mother's main problem in the passage?

    Ⓐ   Her daughters have too many things.

    Ⓑ   Her daughters need more clothes.

    Ⓒ   Her daughters wear the same outfits.

    ●   Her daughters are always fighting.

5   Which sentence spoken by the mother best supports your answer to Question 4?

    ●   *"Why can't you girls just get along?"*

    Ⓑ   *"But choose carefully because you can each only have one outfit."*

    Ⓒ   *"But do you want to each pick a different color?"*

    Ⓓ   *"You both chose these clothes, so you can both wear them."*

6   Read this sentence from the passage.

"Why can't you girls just get along?" she would ask them time and time again.

What does the phrase "time and time again" suggest?

    Ⓐ   That the mother has asked the question for the last time

    Ⓑ   That the mother asks at the same time each day

    ●   That the mother has asked the question many times

    Ⓓ   That the mother asked the question once an hour

7   Where would this passage most likely be found?

Ⓐ   In a book of poems

Ⓑ   In a magazine

Ⓒ   In a science textbook

●   In a book of short stories

8   What most likely happens next in the passage?

Ⓐ   The girls go shopping again

●   The girls go to school looking the same

Ⓒ   The girls put on a different matching outfit

Ⓓ   The girls ask their father for help

9   What happens right after the girls come downstairs for breakfast?

●   They see that they are wearing the same thing.

Ⓑ   They begin to argue.

Ⓒ   They start giggling.

Ⓓ   They get dressed for school.

10   If the passage was given another title, which title would best fit?

Ⓐ   Being Your Best

Ⓑ   How to Shop Well

●   Fighting Over Nothing

Ⓓ   The Magic Dress

11   Explain why you chose the title in Question 10. In your answer, describe how the title you chose tells the theme. Use information from the passage to support your answer.

I chose the title, "Fighting Over Nothing" because what they argue about does not really matter. When the mom said, "Now you can see what your silly arguments have led to," she way describing their arguments as having little to no value.

12   Think about how the girls are always competing with each other. Describe **one** way this competing could be good for them.

One way competing could be good for them is it makes them better.

END OF PRACTICE SET

English Language Arts

Practice Set 2

Reading

Literature Text

Instructions

This set has one passage for you to read. The passage is followed by questions.

Read each question carefully. For each multiple-choice question, fill in the circle for the correct answer. For other types of questions, follow the instructions given. Some of the questions require a written answer. Write your answer on the lines provided.

The Top of the Tower

Toby had a fear of heights. He had carried it with him since he was an infant. As a teenager, his fear had only become worse. He talked to his father about it one day.

"I have had enough Dad," he said. "I would love to go rock climbing with my friends. But every time I get too high, I feel sick."

His dad paused as he thought about his son's problem.

"Well Toby," he said quietly, "I can help you. But you will need to face your fear. Are you ready?"

Toby was quiet for a moment.

"I am ready!" he replied bravely.

Toby's father picked up the keys and walked toward the front door.

"We're going into the city!" his father said.

Toby knew what was coming. Toby lived in Paris, France. Located in the heart of Paris, was one of the world's tallest landmarks. It was the Eiffel Tower. Toby knew that visitors were allowed to climb to the very top. The view overlooked the entire city. Nothing was said between the pair as they drove into the city.

They had arrived at the Eiffel Tower when Toby looked up at it and gasped. His stomach turned over.

"I'm not sure if I can do this," he said nervously.

Toby's father sensed his son's worries.

"Don't worry," he said. "I will be with you every step of the way. This is the day that you beat your fears."

Toby stared up at the giant tower. He took a deep breath as they stepped through the entrance. As his father held his hand, they made their way, step by step, towards the top of the building. Once they reached the top, Toby stepped out from the shadows and onto the ledge.

"Wow, Dad!" he said excitedly as he looked over Paris. The city looked so beautiful from the tower that his fear began to fade. He kept his hand firmly on the tower's metal railing just in case. It felt strong and steady. He still felt a small knot of fear in his stomach, but he told himself that he was fine. Just like the tower, he felt strong and steady.

"I told you there was nothing to worry about," his father said.

1   What does the phrase "heart of" mean in the sentence below?

> **Located in the heart of Paris, was one of the world's tallest landmarks.**

- Ⓐ   Streets of
- Ⓑ   Edge of
- Ⓒ   Center of
- Ⓓ   City of

2   Read this sentence from the passage.

> **Nothing was said between the pair as they drove into the city.**

Why was Toby most likely quiet?

- Ⓐ   He was fighting with his father.
- Ⓑ   He was feeling scared.
- Ⓒ   He was excited.
- Ⓓ   He was having a nap.

3   Based on the second paragraph, what is the main reason Toby wants to change?

- Ⓐ   He does not like being teased.
- Ⓑ   He wants to make his father proud.
- Ⓒ   He is scared that things will get worse.
- Ⓓ   He is tired of missing out on doing things.

4 Describe **two** details from the passage that show that Toby feels nervous about climbing the Eiffel Tower.

1: _He looked up at it and gasped._

2: _I'm not sure if I can do this."_

5 Read this sentence from the passage.

> **As his father held his hand, they made their way, step by step, towards the top of the building.**

What do the words "step by step" suggest?

Ⓐ They moved quite slowly.

Ⓑ They walked a long way.

Ⓒ They raced each other.

Ⓓ They made a lot of noise.

6 Who is telling the story?

Ⓐ Toby

Ⓑ Toby's father

Ⓒ A friend of Toby's

Ⓓ Someone not in the story

7   The main theme of the passage is about –

   Ⓐ   taking chances

   ⬤   overcoming fears

   Ⓒ   making friends

   Ⓓ   asking for help

8   In the second last paragraph, Toby is described as feeling "strong and steady." The word <u>steady</u> probably means that he feels –

   Ⓐ   scared

   Ⓑ   sick

   ⬤   calm

   Ⓓ   joyful

9   Complete these sentences. Write **one** of the words below on each line.

shy   calm   ⟨afraid⟩   amazed

⟨brave⟩   silly   kind   rude

When Toby looks up at the tower, he feels _afraid_ .

When Toby climbs the tower, he is being _brave_ .

10 How do you think Toby feels at the end of the passage? Use details from the passage to explain your answer.

I think Toby feels brave and happy at the end of the passage. "Just like the tower, he felt strong and steady."

11 What is Toby's main problem in the passage? How does Toby overcome the problem? Use details from the passage in your answer.

Toby's main problem in the passage is that he was afraid of heights. Toby overcame the problem by his father helping him go to the top of the Eiffel Tower step by step along the way.

END OF PRACTICE SET

English Language Arts

Practice Set 3

Reading and Writing

Nonfiction Text with Persuasive Writing Task

Instructions

This set has one passage for you to read. The passage is followed by questions.

Read each question carefully. For each multiple-choice question, fill in the circle for the correct answer. For other types of questions, follow the instructions given. Some of the questions require a written answer. Write your answer on the lines provided.

Yard Sales

A yard sale is when you sell items in your front yard. People have yard sales to get rid of unwanted items. It can also be a good way to make some extra money. Here are some tips on how to have a good yard sale.

Finding the Items

1. You need a lot of items to sell. Search your home for all your unwanted items. Make sure everyone in the family joins in. Try to get a large range of items.

2. Clean out the garage or basement. Many people have a store of old stuff somewhere. Offer to clean up this area. As you do, collect everything you think you can sell.

3. Ask other people you know to join in. Many people have junk lying around they want to get rid of. They may be happy to give it to you to sell.

Setting It Up

1. Collect everything you have to sell. It is a good idea to make everything look neat and tidy. If you have clothes, wash them and hang them up. They may not be new clothes, but they'll have to look fresh and clean if you want people to buy them. Clean and dust all the items so they look their best.

2. Set up tables in your front yard to place all the items on. If you are placing items on the ground, put them on a sheet or blanket.

3. People will need to know how much each item is. Put a sticker on each item and write the price on it.

4. Collect some change. People will often pay in notes. Make sure you have plenty of coins to give as change.

Getting a Crowd

1. You want lots of people to come to your yard sale. Here are some things you should do:

- Tell all your friends
- Put notices on notice boards
- Put up flyers
- Put an ad in the local newspaper
- Put a sign at the end of your street

2. Make it easy for people to find the yard sale. Put balloons at the end of your street and in your front yard.

Time to Sell

1. Now it is time to sell your items. Remember that you are selling things you don't really want. Don't try to sell your items for too much. Be open to haggling too. Many people will want a bargain and may not want to pay what you think it's worth. If people suggest a lower price, take it! If people are thinking about buying something, make them a deal.

2. If items are not selling, lower the prices. It is better to sell items for something than to have to pack them all up again.

Popular Yard Sale Items
children's toys
clothes
building materials
furniture
kitchen items
books and movies

1   Read this sentence from the passage.

People often have yard sales to get rid of unwanted items.

What does the word <u>unwanted</u> mean?

Ⓐ   Less wanted

Ⓑ   Used to be wanted

Ⓒ   More wanted

●   Not wanted

2   Why should you put balloons in your front yard?

Ⓐ   So people feel good about buying

Ⓑ   So you can sell them

●   So people can find your yard sale

Ⓓ   So you can put prices on them

3   If the passage was given another title, which of these would best fit?

Ⓐ   How to Make Money

●   How to Hold a Yard Sale

Ⓒ   The Amazing Yard Sale

Ⓓ   Cleaning Up Your House

4 Read this sentence from the passage.

It is a good idea to make everything look neat and tidy.

Which word means the opposite of <u>neat</u>?

Ⓐ Messy

Ⓑ Clean

Ⓒ Dirty

Ⓓ Nice

5 Which section of the passage describes how to let people know about your yard sale?

Ⓐ Finding the Items

Ⓑ Setting It Up

Ⓒ Getting a Crowd

Ⓓ Time to Sell

6 According to the passage, which of the following should you do first?

Ⓐ Set up tables

Ⓑ Clean all the items

Ⓒ Put stickers on the items

Ⓓ Lower the prices

7   How does the information in the table help the reader?

    Ⓐ   It explains how much money can be made.

    ⬤   It shows what sort of items to collect.

    Ⓒ   It shows how to price items.

    Ⓓ   It explains why you should have a yard sale.

8   Which phrase from "Time to Sell" best helps you understand the meaning of <u>haggling</u>? Tick the box of the phrase you have selected.

    ☐   "now it is time"

    ☐   "things you don't really want"

    ☐   "many people"

    ☑   "suggest a lower price"

    ☐   "thinking about buying"

9   Describe **two** things the art in the passage helps you understand.

1: The two things that help me is the yard sale sign

2: and the items.

10 Draw lines to match each sentence in the first paragraph with its main purpose.

A yard sale is when you sell items in your front yard.	to give a second reason for having a yard sale
People have yard sales to get rid of unwanted items.	to tell what a yard sale is
It can also be a good way to make some extra money.	to give the main reason for having a yard sale
Here are some tips on how to have a good yard sale.	to tell what the passage is about

11 In "Finding the Items," the author suggests that you ask other people to join in. Explain why you think this would be a good idea. Use information from the passage to support your response.

Asking other people to join helps make more money.

12 Sort the list of things to do below into things that would be best to do in the week before your yard sale and things that would be best to do on the day of your yard sale. Write **three** of the items in each column.

put up flyers   put balloons up   set up the tables

tell your friends   put a sign in your street   run a newspaper ad

The Week Before Your Yard Sale	On the Day of Your Yard Sale

13 Do you think that holding a yard sale is a good way for young people to make money on the weekend? Explain why or why not. In your answer, include **three** reasons to support your opinion. You can use information from the passage and your own opinions and ideas.

Young people should not have a yard sale because it's not safe for strangers to be around; dangerous people could come and steal your child; and young people might not know the true value/worth of items.

END OF PRACTICE SET

English Language Arts

Practice Set 4

Reading and Writing

Nonfiction Text with Informative Writing Task

Instructions

This set has one passage for you to read. The passage is followed by questions.

Read each question carefully. For each multiple-choice question, fill in the circle for the correct answer. For other types of questions, follow the instructions given. Some of the questions require a written answer. Write your answer on the lines provided.

Summer Lemonade

Lemonade is one of the most popular summer drinks in the United States. It is refreshing and helps you to cool down during the hot summer months. Lemonade is available in most stores and can be purchased as a premade drink. These brands are often made with added sugar and other chemicals. These ingredients often make the drink unhealthy. So we're going to make a healthy homemade lemonade!

To make our own lemonade at home we'll need the right ingredients. You will need 1 cup of sugar, 6 lemons, 1 cup of boiling water, and 4 cups of cold water. You will also need a saucepan and a large pitcher.

Step 1
Start by placing the sugar in a saucepan. Then add the boiling water and heat the mixture gently.

Step 2
Extract the juice from your 6 lemons. You can use a juicer. Or you can squeeze them by hand. Add the lemon juice to the water and sugar mixture.

Step 3
Pour the mixture into a pitcher. Then take your 4 cups of cold water and add these to the pitcher. This will cool the mixture down and make it ready to refrigerate. The amount of cold water that you add will affect the strength of the lemonade. You can add more water if you like it weaker.

Step 4
Refrigerate the mixture for 30 or 40 minutes. Taste your lemonade mixture. If it is too sweet, add a little more lemon juice. If it is too strong, add some more water. If it is too sour, add some more sugar.

Step 5
You are now ready to serve your lemonade. Pour it into a glass with ice and a slice of lemon.

Now that you know how to make lemonade, why not use this new skill to make some money on the weekend? Make a nice big batch of lemonade and start a lemonade stand in your front yard. Here are some tips for setting up a good lemonade stand.

1. Make sure you have a good spot. You're usually not allowed to set up stands in public places like parks, so you'll need to do it in your yard. But it's best if you live in a spot where plenty of people will walk past. If your home is not right, consider asking a friend who lives in a better spot to help you. Then you can set up the stand at your friend's house.

2. Get your stand noticed. You want your stand to be easy to spot. Take the time to paint a colorful banner or to put up signs. You can also add things like streamers and balloons. You could also put signs up at the end of your street. Then people will know that fresh lemonade is just around the corner.

3. Choose the right price. You need to make sure you aren't charging too much for your lemonade. It's also easiest if you don't need to worry about giving change. Set your price to $1, $2, or $3. You should also be willing to do deals. If someone wants to buy more than one, offer them a special deal.

4. You want people to want to drink your lemonade, so make sure you present it nicely. You can add a few lemon wedges to the container to make it look nice and fresh. You can also place lemons around your stand as decorations. You should also cover the table you are using with a nice tablecloth. The nicer your stand looks, the more people will want to buy your product.

5. Add other products. Do you have a friend who makes delicious cupcakes or amazing banana bread? Invite them to join in. You can sell treats to go with your fresh lemonade and make even more money.

1   Read this sentence from the passage.

> **Lemonade is available in most stores and can be purchased as a premade drink.**

What does the word <u>purchased</u> mean?

Ⓐ   Made

Ⓑ   Found

Ⓒ   Bought

Ⓓ   Eaten

2   What would be the best way to improve how the information in paragraph 2 is presented?

Ⓐ   Add bullet points

Ⓑ   Add a diagram

Ⓒ   Add a chart

Ⓓ   Add a graph

3   What is the main purpose of the passage?

Ⓐ   To instruct

Ⓑ   To entertain

Ⓒ   To inform

Ⓓ   To persuade

4   In which step is the sugar first needed? Circle the correct step.

Step 1   Step 2   Step 3   Step 4   Step 5

5   As it is used below, which word means the opposite of <u>weaker</u>?

You can add more water if you like it weaker.

Ⓐ   Nicer

Ⓑ   Stronger

Ⓒ   Thinner

Ⓓ   Colder

6   Complete the diagram by writing **one** of the sentences below in each box.

Add water.   Add lemon juice.   Add sugar.

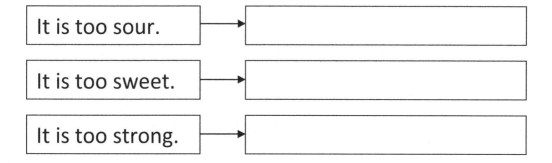

Problem with the Lemonade   How to Solve the Problem

It is too sour.	→	
It is too sweet.	→	
It is too strong.	→	

7   According to the passage, why is homemade lemonade better than lemonade from a store?

   Ⓐ   It lasts longer.

   Ⓑ   It is cheaper.

   Ⓒ   It is better for you.

   Ⓓ   It is easier to make.

8   What is the main purpose of the first paragraph?

   Ⓐ   To describe how to make lemonade

   Ⓑ   To encourage people to want to make lemonade

   Ⓒ   To tell what lemonade is made from

   Ⓓ   To explain where to get lemonade from

9   Based on the information in the passage, describe **two** ways asking a friend to help with your lemonade stand would help you.

   1: _____

   _____

   2: _____

   _____

10   Write the name of each item used to make the lemonade in the order they are added.

boiling water   cold water   lemons   sugar

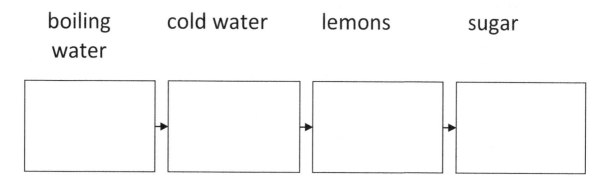

11   Do you feel it would be worth it to set up a lemonade stand? Explain why or why not. Use information from the passage to support your response.

_____

_____

_____

_____

_____

_____

_____

12 The passage gives an idea for making money on the weekend. Write an article for your school newspaper suggesting that students set up a lemonade stand on the weekend.

In your response, be sure to
- describe how students can make money
- tell some of the benefits of a lemonade stand
- give some advice for making the event a success
- use details from the passage

_____

_____

_____

_____

_____

_____

_____

_____

_____

_____

_____

_____

_____

_____

_____

_____

_____

_____

_____

_____

_____

_____

_____

_____

_____

_____

_____

END OF PRACTICE SET

English Language Arts

Practice Set 5

Reading and Writing

Literature Text with Narrative Writing Task

Instructions
This set has one passage for you to read. The passage is followed by questions. Read each question carefully. For each multiple-choice question, fill in the circle for the correct answer. For other types of questions, follow the instructions given. Some of the questions require a written answer. Write your answer on the lines provided.

A Special Day

Dear Uncle Yuri,

Today was quite an amazing day for me. It was the day that my father returned home from overseas. He had been away from us for over a year. He was chosen to work on a special research project in London. He and his team were working on a new way to make recycled paper products. It would use less water and energy and be better for the environment. Although we were proud of him, we longed for the day when he would wake up under the same roof as us. We had missed him more than words could ever say. Now the day had finally arrived. He had worked hard and it was time for him to return home.

Mom woke us at 6 a.m. to head to the airport. My father's flight was due in at 9:30. "We don't want to be late!" she kept saying as she woke everyone up. She had no need to remind me! I quickly dressed, washed, and made my way downstairs for breakfast. I could not take my eyes off the clock all morning. Time was going so slowly. When the clock struck 8:45, my mom told us all it was time to go. We all raced to the car and made our way quickly to the airport.

We arrived just after 9 and hurried to the terminal to wait. But 9:30 came and went and our father's flight had still not arrived. Another 10 minutes went by, and I started pacing up and down. I kept asking Mom where he was. She just kept smiling and saying he'd be there soon. I searched the crowds of people, hoping to see his familiar face. I stood as tall as I could to try and see every person coming through the gate.

Then suddenly a gap appeared in the crowd and a tall shadow emerged. There was my father standing before me. He dropped his bags to the floor and swept my sister and I up in his arms. "I've missed you so much," he said through tears of joy. We all cried together. I never want my father to ever let me go.

Today was pretty perfect.

Holly

1   Read this sentence from the letter.

I could not take my eyes off the clock all morning.

This sentence shows that Holly was –

Ⓐ   worried

Ⓑ   excited

Ⓒ   bored

Ⓓ   patient

2   Why does Holly most likely say that she doesn't need to be reminded not to be late?

Ⓐ   She does not care if they are late.

Ⓑ   She knows that the plane will be late.

Ⓒ   She would never want to be late.

Ⓓ   She thinks that they will be late anyway.

3   The second paragraph starts with the sentence "Mom woke us at 6 a.m. to head to the airport." How is the second paragraph mainly organized?

Ⓐ   A problem is described and then a solution is given.

Ⓑ   Events are described in the order they occur.

Ⓒ   Facts are given to support an argument.

Ⓓ   A question is asked and then answered.

4   The reader can tell that Holly's father –

    Ⓐ   missed his family very much

    Ⓑ   wants to go overseas again

    Ⓒ   is surprised to be home

    Ⓓ   thinks his kids have grown up a lot

5   How does Holly most likely feel while waiting at the airport?

    Ⓐ   Surprised

    Ⓑ   Anxious

    Ⓒ   Calm

    Ⓓ   Bored

6   Based on your answer to Question 5, describe **two** details given about Holly that show how she feels while waiting at the airport.

    1: _____

    _____

    2: _____

    _____

7   Which sentence from the letter best shows how Holly feels about having her father home?

Ⓐ   *There was my father standing before me.*

Ⓑ   *He dropped his bags to the floor and swept my sister and I up in his arms.*

Ⓒ   *We all cried together.*

Ⓓ   *I never want my father to ever let me go.*

8   Read this sentence from the letter.

We had missed him more than words could ever say.

Which literary device is used in this sentence?

Ⓐ   Imagery, using details to create an image or picture

Ⓑ   Hyperbole, using exaggeration to make a point

Ⓒ   Simile, comparing two items using the words "like" or "as"

Ⓓ   Symbolism, using an object to stand for something else

9   Which sentence from the letter best explains why Holly is looking forward to seeing her father so much?

Ⓐ   *Today was quite an amazing day for me.*

Ⓑ   *He had been away from us for over a year.*

Ⓒ   *My father's flight was due in at 9:30.*

Ⓓ   *Time was going so slowly.*

10   The photograph in the passage mainly helps show that the airport was –

Ⓐ   clean

Ⓑ   loud

Ⓒ   crowded

Ⓓ   cold

11   Read this sentence from the passage.

> **He dropped his bags to the floor and swept my sister and I up in his arms.**

Explain what the father's actions in this sentence show about how he feels.

_____

_____

_____

_____

_____

_____

12   The passage tells about the first time Holly saw her father again after he was away for a year. Think about what might happen when the family gets home. Pretend you are Holly and write another letter to Uncle Yuri. In this letter, describe the first night with your father home.

_____

_____

_____

_____

_____

_____

_____

_____

_____

_____

_____

_____

_____

_____

_____

_____

_____

_____

_____

_____

_____

_____

_____

_____

_____

_____

_____

END OF PRACTICE SET

English Language Arts

Practice Set 6

Reading

Literature Text

Instructions

This set has one passage for you to read. The passage is followed by questions.

Read each question carefully. For each multiple-choice question, fill in the circle for the correct answer. For other types of questions, follow the instructions given. Some of the questions require a written answer. Write your answer on the lines provided.

The Wiggly Worm

The worm is one of nature's
most wonderful of creatures,
as it slinks beneath the soil,
with all its special features.

The worm is an explorer,
of both soft and well-worn land,
on a journey through the landscape,
unearthing stones, loose earth, and sand.

Though they barely see above the grass,
they see all beneath the ground,
hiding amongst the flower beds,
as they wiggle round and round.

Their bodies are long and slender
and as light as summer's breeze,
gilding shapes beneath the surface,
with slow and steady ease.

They're the envy of the rhino,
the hippopotamus, and ape,
and all the other animals that lack
one single beautiful shape.

So when you see the wiggly worm,
smile at his simple form,
and ponder his adventures,
in the earth all wet and warm.

1   Read this line from the poem.

they see all beneath the ground,

Which word means the opposite of <u>beneath</u>?

Ⓐ   Below

Ⓑ   Above

Ⓒ   Far

Ⓓ   Along

2   Write the **two** words that best complete the sentence on the lines.

scary   amazing   ugly   boring

dirty   beautiful   sad   lonely

The poet would most likely describe worms as _____ and

_____.

3   What is the rhyme pattern of each stanza of the poem?

Ⓐ   The second and fourth lines rhyme.

Ⓑ   There are two pairs of rhyming lines.

Ⓒ   The first and last lines rhyme.

Ⓓ   None of the lines rhyme.

4 Which line from the poem contains a simile?

Ⓐ   *as it slinks beneath the soil,*

Ⓑ   *hiding amongst the flower beds,*

Ⓒ   *and as light as summer's breeze,*

Ⓓ   *So when you see the wiggly worm,*

5 Which words from the poem describe what a worm looks like?

Ⓐ   *soft and well-worn*

Ⓑ   *long and slender*

Ⓒ   *slow and steady*

Ⓓ   *wet and warm*

6 Select **all** the lines below that contain alliteration.

☐   *most wonderful of creatures,*

☐   *with all its special features.*

☐   *The worm is an explorer,*

☐   *they see all beneath the ground,*

☐   *with slow and steady ease.*

☐   *and ponder his adventures,*

☐   *in the earth all wet and warm.*

7   The poet describes worms as explorers. What makes a worm like an explorer? In your answer, explain what worms explore. Use information from the poem to support your answer.

_____

_____

_____

_____

_____

8   The poet tries to get readers to feel like worms are interesting and special. Do you feel that the poet is successful? Explain why or why not.

_____

_____

_____

_____

9   According to the poem, why is the worm the envy of the rhino,
hippopotamus, and ape? Explain what the worm has that these animals do
not.

_____

_____

_____

_____

_____

_____

10   What does the poet mainly want readers to learn from the poem?

Ⓐ   Where worms can be found

Ⓑ   Why worms are useful

Ⓒ   How interesting worms are

Ⓓ   How worms are able to move

END OF PRACTICE SET

English Language Arts

Practice Set 7

Reading

Literature Text

Instructions

This set has one passage for you to read. The passage is followed by questions.

Read each question carefully. For each multiple-choice question, fill in the circle for the correct answer. For other types of questions, follow the instructions given. Some of the questions require a written answer. Write your answer on the lines provided.

The Bumble Bee

Yellow and black with a set of tiny wings,
I busily buzz around the land,
And boast a mighty sting!

I do not care for fame or money,
I do not wish to harm,
I just live for making honey!

This beekeeper holds up honeycomb that has been made in the hive. The honey is extracted, or taken out, from the honeycomb. Bees can sting, so this beekeeper wears a special bee suit to keep him safe. Bees usually only sting when they are afraid of something. The best way to be safe from bees is simply to leave them alone!

1   According to the poem, what does the bee enjoy most?

    Ⓐ   Being famous

    Ⓑ   Being rich

    Ⓒ   Making honey

    Ⓓ   Stinging people

2   Read this line from the poem.

I busily buzz around the land,

Which literary device is used in this line?

    Ⓐ   Alliteration

    Ⓑ   Simile

    Ⓒ   Metaphor

    Ⓓ   Imagery

3   What is the rhyme pattern of each stanza of the poem?

    Ⓐ   Every line rhymes.

    Ⓑ   The first and second lines rhyme.

    Ⓒ   The first and last lines rhyme.

    Ⓓ   None of the lines rhyme.

4 Onomatopoeia is when a word sounds like what it describes. Which word from the poem is an example of onomatopoeia?

Ⓐ   *black*

Ⓑ   *wings*

Ⓒ   *buzz*

Ⓓ   *sting*

5 In the line below, what does the word <u>mighty</u> mean?

And boast a mighty sting!

Ⓐ   Scary

Ⓑ   Strange

Ⓒ   Naughty

Ⓓ   Great

6 Which sentence from the caption best supports the idea that bees do not wish to harm?

Ⓐ   *This beekeeper holds up honeycomb that has been made in the hive.*

Ⓑ   *The honey is extracted, or taken out, from the honeycomb.*

Ⓒ   *Bees can sting, so this beekeeper wears a special bee suit to keep him safe.*

Ⓓ   *Bees usually only sting when they are afraid of something.*

7   What does the photograph help readers understand? Explain your answer.

_____

_____

_____

_____

_____

_____

8   Complete the diagram below by listing **three** facts the author gives about bees.

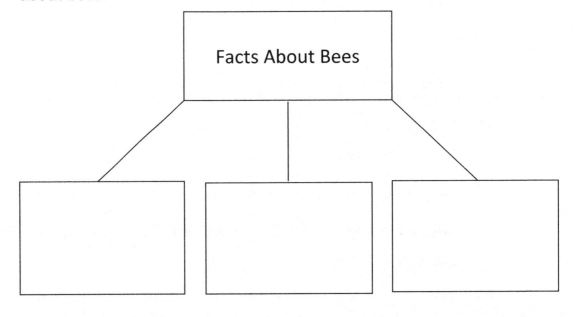

9 While bees can be dangerous, do you think most poeple need to fear bees? Explain your answer.

_____

_____

_____

_____

_____

10 The poem is written from the point of view of a bee. How does this point of view affect the poem? Explain whether or not it helps readers take the poem seriously. Use details from the poem to support your answer.

_____

_____

_____

_____

_____

END OF PRACTICE SET

English Language Arts

Practice Set 8

Reading and Writing

Nonfiction Text with Informative Writing Task

Instructions

This set has one passage for you to read. The passage is followed by questions.

Read each question carefully. For each multiple-choice question, fill in the circle for the correct answer. For other types of questions, follow the instructions given. Some of the questions require a written answer. Write your answer on the lines provided.

A Letter to My Favorite Author

July 1, 2013

Dear Simeon,

I am writing to tell you what a huge fan I am of your work. I have enjoyed your books since I was eight years old. I read a story in the newspaper that said you were ill. It made me feel sad. I wanted to write just to tell you how much I like your work. And that I hope you feel better soon too!

My love for your work began with your first book. *The Singing Swordfish* was so well-written. The pictures also helped to bring your words to life. I laughed so hard I cried the first time I read the book! From then on, I was hooked on your every word. I cannot imagine a better children's author existing anywhere else in the world. If there is one, I would certainly like to know about them too! If I had to choose which of your books was my favorite, it would be *The Shining Light*. That story was such an adventure from start to finish. Your book *Rainy Day* is also a favorite. It made me think a lot. And of course, I love *Just Lazing Around* as well. It always makes me laugh.

I hope that you feel better soon. You have given so much joy to so many people. Take care and thank you for all of the memories and moments of joy that you have given me.

Yours sincerely,

Kyle Harper

1   Read this sentence from the letter.

From then on, I was hooked on your every word.

What does the phrase "hooked on" mean?

Ⓐ   Very keen on

Ⓑ   Confused by

Ⓒ   Bent

Ⓓ   Owned

2   Read this sentence from the letter.

I cannot imagine a better children's author existing anywhere else in the world.

Which word means about the same as <u>existing</u>?

Ⓐ   Living

Ⓑ   Writing

Ⓒ   Working

Ⓓ   Thinking

3 According to the letter, why does Kyle decide to write to Simeon?

Ⓐ He is asked to by his mother.

Ⓑ He wants to be sent a free book.

Ⓒ He wants her to write another book.

Ⓓ He reads that she is ill.

4 Based on your answer to Question 3, choose **two** sentences from the first paragraph that support your answer. Circle the **two** sentences below. Then explain why you chose those sentences.

> I am writing to tell you what a huge fan I am of your work. I have enjoyed your books since I was eight years old. I read a story in the newspaper that said you were ill. It made me feel sad. I wanted to write just to tell you how much I like your work. And that I hope you feel better soon too!

_____

_____

_____

_____

_____

5   Complete the chart by writing **one** book from the list below in each space.

The Singing Swordfish   *The Shining Light*
Rainy Day   *Just Lazing Around*

Favorite Book:	
First Book Read:	

6   The reader can tell that Kyle –

Ⓐ   no longer reads Simeon's books

Ⓑ   wants to be a writer someday

Ⓒ   has read many of Simeon's books

Ⓓ   started reading because he was ill

7   What is the first paragraph mainly about?

Ⓐ   Why Kyle is writing to Simeon

Ⓑ   When Kyle started reading Simeon's books

Ⓒ   Which book of Simeon's is Kyle's favorite

Ⓓ   How Kyle reads the newspaper

8 Which part of the letter tells who wrote the letter?

Ⓐ Date

Ⓑ Greeting

Ⓒ Closing

Ⓓ Body

9 Describe **two** reasons that Kyle liked the book *The Singing Swordfish*.

1: _____

2: _____

10 Do you think Simeon would feel good after reading the letter? Explain why or why not.

_____

_____

_____

_____

_____

_____

11 In the letter, you can tell that Kyle enjoys reading books. Think about what Kyle enjoys about reading books and what he gains from it. Think about what you enjoy reading about books and what you gain from it. Write an essay that explains why reading books is a popular hobby and why people enjoy reading books. You can use information from the passage, your own ideas, or your own research in your essay.

_____

_____

_____

_____

_____

_____

_____

_____

_____

_____

_____

_____

_____

END OF PRACTICE SET

English Language Arts

Practice Set 9

Reading and Writing

Nonfiction Text with Persuasive Writing Task

Instructions

This set has one passage for you to read. The passage is followed by questions.

Read each question carefully. For each multiple-choice question, fill in the circle for the correct answer. For other types of questions, follow the instructions given. Some of the questions require a written answer. Write your answer on the lines provided.

No Time to Talk

May 23, 2013

Dear Principal Becker,

I understand that school is meant for learning. It is important to have good reading skills and to be able to solve math problems. But I think school is also important for another reason. It helps people learn to get along with others.

It may seem like lunchtime is not important. After all, I spend most lunchtimes just chatting to my friends. But this activity is more important than it looks.

I am learning how to get along with others. I am learning how to solve problems. I am finding out new things from people, and realizing my mistakes. I am learning how to stand up for myself. I am learning how to say sorry. These are all important skills to learn.

My problem is that the time for lunch and our other breaks keep getting shorter. I know this is happening so we can spend more time in class learning. But please do not forget that we are also learning in our lunchtimes. We are learning people skills. It is important that we have enough time to spend with our friends.

I ask that you consider making our lunch break longer. A little more time spent with friends each day would benefit everybody.

Best,

Simone Anderson

1 Read this sentence from the letter.

> **My problem is that the time for lunch and our other breaks keep getting shorter.**

What does the word <u>shorter</u> mean?

Ⓐ Less short

Ⓑ The most short

Ⓒ More short

Ⓓ The least short

2 What does the word <u>benefit</u> mean in the sentence below?

> **A little more time spent with friends each day would benefit everybody.**

Ⓐ Change

Ⓑ Help

Ⓒ Interest

Ⓓ Harm

3 According to the letter, what does Simone learn at lunchtime?

Ⓐ Math skills

Ⓑ Reading skills

Ⓒ People skills

Ⓓ Drawing skills

4   Why did Simone write the letter?

   Ⓐ   To persuade the principal to do something

   Ⓑ   To entertain the principal

   Ⓒ   To show the principal her writing skills

   Ⓓ   To teach the principal how to do something

5   Which sentence best shows the main idea of the letter?

   Ⓐ   *I understand that school is meant for learning.*

   Ⓑ   *It may seem like lunchtime is not important.*

   Ⓒ   *After all, I spend most lunchtimes just chatting to my friends.*

   Ⓓ   *It is important that we have enough time to spend with our friends.*

6   What is the paragraph below mostly about?

> **I am learning how to get along with others. I am learning how to solve problems. I am finding out new things from people, and realizing my mistakes. I am learning how to stand up for myself. I am learning how to say sorry. These are all important skills to learn.**

   Ⓐ   What Simone learns at lunchtime

   Ⓑ   How long lunchtime lasts for

   Ⓒ   What skills students should be taught

   Ⓓ   What problems Simone has each day

7   Look at the web below.

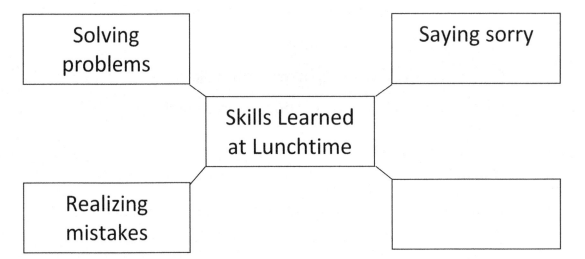

Which of these best completes the web? Write your answer in the web.

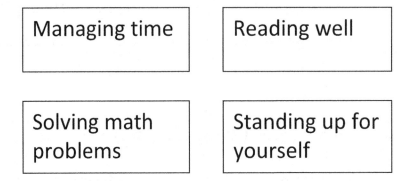

8   Which statement is most likely true about Simone?

Ⓐ   She writes a lot of letters to the principal.

Ⓑ   She spends a lot of time in class talking.

Ⓒ   She enjoys spending time with her friends.

Ⓓ   She wishes that her friends were nicer.

9   What are the main benefits of increasing the length of the lunch break?
Use information from the passage to support your answer.

_____

_____

_____

_____

_____

_____

_____

_____

_____

_____

_____

_____

_____

10 Two more benefits of having a longer lunch break are given below. For each benefit, write a paragraph that could be added to the letter. In the paragraph, describe the benefit and use it to help persuade the principal.

Benefit 1: Students need time to rest between classes.

_____

_____

_____

_____

_____

Benefit 2: Students will behave better during class if they are allowed time to have fun between classes.

_____

_____

_____

_____

_____

END OF PRACTICE SET

English Language Arts

Practice Set 10

Reading and Writing

Literature Text with Narrative Writing Task

Instructions

This set has one passage for you to read. The passage is followed by questions.

Read each question carefully. For each multiple-choice question, fill in the circle for the correct answer. For other types of questions, follow the instructions given. Some of the questions require a written answer. Write your answer on the lines provided.

The Troublemaker

 Kevin had always been known for playing tricks. As he got older, his tricks got worse. Over time, everyone began to know Kevin as a troublemaker. Kevin enjoyed all of the attention. He almost felt famous for his tricks.

One day, he was at his friend Jason's house playing hide and seek. Kevin told Jason to hide from the others in his basement. Jason opened the door and started down the steps. Kevin quickly locked the basement door behind him. Kevin put the key into his pocket and skipped away.

Jason called out to his friends. He couldn't hear a reply, so he called out a little louder. He rattled the doorknob hoping it would open. Then he began banging on the door. Jason's friends heard the sound and raced to the door. They called out to let Jason know they would get him out soon. Jason's friend Max pushed on the door as hard as he could. But the door would not budge.

Eventually, Jason's mother heard the noise and came downstairs. She unlocked the door with a spare key and hugged her son as he ran out.

"Who did this?" she asked firmly.

Kevin smiled and put his hand in the air. Jason's mother sighed.

 "You seem very proud, Kevin," she said. "But what you don't realize is that being well-known for something isn't always a good thing. Maybe once you were thought of as funny, but now you're just becoming nasty."

Kevin's shoulders slumped.

"I guess so," he whispered. "I just thought it would be funny. I didn't mean to hurt anybody. But I guess nobody is laughing, are they?"

Kevin decided he would have to be more careful about the jokes he chose to play on his friends.

1   Read these sentences from the passage.

> **Jason's friend Max pushed on the door as hard as he could. But the door would not budge.**

What does the word <u>budge</u> mean in the sentence?

Ⓐ   Break

Ⓑ   Bend

Ⓒ   Move

Ⓓ   Listen

2   Circle the **two** words from the passage that have about the same meaning.

friends	famous	tricks
nasty	proud	well-known
funny	rattled	laughing

3   Who is the main character in the passage?

Ⓐ   Kevin

Ⓑ   Jason's mother

Ⓒ   Jason

Ⓓ   Max

4   Read this sentence from the passage.

Kevin put the key into his pocket and skipped away.

What does the word <u>skipped</u> suggest about Kevin?

Ⓐ   He moved slowly.

Ⓑ   He was happy.

Ⓒ   He moved quietly.

Ⓓ   He was angry.

5   Read the list of the mother's actions in the story. Order the actions from first to last by writing the numbers 1, 2, 3, and 4 on the lines.

_____   She asks who locked Jason in the basement.

_____   She lets Jason out of the basement.

_____   She explains to Kevin why he should not play tricks.

_____   She hears a noise coming from the basement.

6   Which word best describes the trick that Kevin plays on Jason?

Ⓐ   Funny

Ⓑ   Mean

Ⓒ   Strange

Ⓓ   Silly

7   What is the second paragraph mostly about?

   Ⓐ   Why Kevin plays tricks

   Ⓑ   How children should not play in basements

   Ⓒ   A trick that Kevin plays on a friend

   Ⓓ   How a boy learns why he shouldn't play tricks

8   Which word describes how Jason feels while he is locked in the basement?

   Ⓐ   Calm

   Ⓑ   Bored

   Ⓒ   Angry

   Ⓓ   Frightened

9   Choose the **two** sentences from the third paragraph that best support your answer to Question 8. Tick **two** boxes below to show your choices.

☐   Jason called out to his friends.

☐   He couldn't hear a reply, so he called out a little louder.

☐   He rattled the doorknob hoping it would open.

☐   Then he began banging on the door.

☐   Jason's friends heard the sound and raced to the door.

☐   They called out to let Jason know they would get him out soon.

☐   Jason's friend Max pushed on the door as hard as he could.

☐   But the door would not budge.

10   What lesson do you think Kevin learns? Use information from the passage to support your answer.

_____

_____

_____

_____

_____

11   Do you think Kevin will keep playing jokes in the future? Explain why or why not. Use information from the passage to support your answer.

_____

_____

_____

_____

_____

12   In the story, Kevin plays a trick that upsets Jason. Write a story that describes the events from Jason's point of view. Tell how Jason gets locked in the basement, how he feels while he is there, and how he feels after getting out.

_____

_____

_____

_____

_____

_____

_____

_____

_____

_____

_____

_____

_____

_____

_____

_____

_____

_____

_____

_____

_____

_____

_____

_____

_____

_____

END OF PRACTICE SET

_____

English Language Arts

Practice Set 11

Writing

Research, Writing Process, and Writing Conventions

Instructions

The first four questions in this set are writing or research tasks. Read the information and then answer the questions.

This set also has short passages that contain errors or opportunities for improvement. Read each passage and answer the questions that follow it. For each multiple-choice question, fill in the circle for the correct answer. For other types of questions, follow the instructions given.

A student is writing a research paper about sweat bees. He found the source below. Read the source. Then answer the following two questions.

Sweat bees are common throughout North America. There are over 1,000 species found in North America. They are named for their habit of landing on people and licking the sweat from the skin. The bees do this to take in the salt in the sweat.

Bees in this family are small to medium sized, ranging from 4 to 10 mm. They generally are black or brownish in color. However, there are species of sweat bees that are bright metallic green and some that have brassy yellow or red markings. Males tend to have yellow faces. Sweat bees build nests in clay soil, sandy banks, and cavities in weeds or shrubs.

1   Circle the sentence from the source that explains why the bees are known as sweat bees.

2   Write a list of details the student could include in the research paper to help readers identify sweat bees.

1. _____

2. _____

3. _____

4. _____

5. _____

The following is part of an opinion article a student is writing for the school newspaper. Read the paragraph. Then answer the following two questions.

I've seen cars driving past the school far too fast. There are lots of kids standing out there waiting for parents or waiting for buses. Others walk or ride home and need to cross the road. It's very dangerous and something needs to be done. There should be more signs to make sure drivers know to slow down. There should also be more teachers to help make sure kids cross the road safely.

3   Write a sentence or two that could be used to start the paragraph. The sentences should state the main idea of the paragraph.

_____

_____

_____

4   The student wants to add more details to support the idea that the situation is very dangerous. List **two** more details the student could add to the opinion article.

1. _____

_____

2. _____

_____

The passage below contains errors. The words or phrases that are incorrect are underlined. For each word or phrase underlined, answer the question below.

Dear Annie,

I hope you are well. I'm a little worried about how I am going in math class. I can do the geometry quite <u>easy</u>. For some reason, shapes just make <u>cents</u> to me. But a lot of the algebra problems just look like weird strings of numbers and symbols.

As you know, <u>mine</u> brother Kevin is quite a whiz at math. I asked him for some help, <u>and</u> he's not very good at explaining things simply. In fact, he really just confused me even more! Mom is going to ask if Miss Bert will tutor me during lunch <u>tomorow</u>. I really <u>hoping</u> I can figure this out soon. It's getting stressful and I really want to do better.

Bye for now,

Alex

5   Which of these should replace <u>easy</u>?

    Ⓐ   easier

    Ⓑ   easily

    Ⓒ   easiness

    Ⓓ   easiest

6   Which of these should replace <u>cents</u>?

    Ⓐ   sents

    Ⓑ   scents

    Ⓒ   sense

    Ⓓ   cense

7   Which of these should replace <u>mine</u>?

    Ⓐ   I

    Ⓑ   I'm

    Ⓒ   me

    Ⓓ   my

8   Which of these should replace <u>and</u>?

    Ⓐ   but

    Ⓑ   if

    Ⓒ   so

    Ⓓ   yet

9   What is the correct way to spell <u>tomorow</u>? Write your answer below.

_____

10   Which of these should replace <u>hoping</u>?

    Ⓐ   hope

    Ⓑ   hopes

    Ⓒ   hoped

    Ⓓ   hopeful

The passage below contains errors. The words or phrases that are incorrect are underlined. For each word or phrase underlined, answer the question below.

The Amazing Amazon

The Amazon River is the <u>secend</u> longest river in the world. Only the Nile River in Africa is longer. The Amazon River has a massive basin of about 3 million square miles. It has the <u>most large</u> basin of any river in the world. In fact, about 20 percent of the <u>worlds</u> total river water is in the Amazon.

The Amazon River is located deep in the rainforests of <u>south america</u>. One of the most <u>intresting</u> things about the river is that there is no point at which the river has a bridge across it. This is because the river flows mainly <u>threw</u> deep rainforests, and there are few towns on the river.

11   Which of these should replace <u>secend</u>?

    Ⓐ   secand

    Ⓑ   second

    Ⓒ   seccend

    Ⓓ   seccond

12   Which of these should replace <u>most large</u>?

    Ⓐ   larger

    Ⓑ   largest

    Ⓒ   more large

    Ⓓ   most largest

13   Which of these should replace <u>worlds</u>?

   Ⓐ   world's

   Ⓑ   worlds'

   Ⓒ   World's

   Ⓓ   Worlds'

14   What is the correct way to capitalize <u>south america</u>? Write your answer below.

   _____

15   What is the correct way to spell <u>intresting</u>? Write your answer below.

   _____

16   Which of these should replace <u>threw</u>?

   Ⓐ   thru

   Ⓑ   though

   Ⓒ   thought

   Ⓓ   through

The passage below contains errors. The words or phrases that are incorrect are underlined. For each word or phrase underlined, answer the question below.

Not So Simple

The donkey <u>were</u> wandering across the farmstead. All of a sudden, he heard the chirp of a grasshopper. The donkey <u>followwed</u> the sound until he saw the grasshopper. He asked the grasshopper how he made such a wonderful sound. The grasshopper explained that he lived off the dew. Then he hopped away. Not many people realize that grasshoppers can also fly. The donkey decided that he was going to eat dew until he could sing.

The donkey <u>eated</u> nothing but dew for weeks. He still didn't sound anything like the grasshopper. He was also starting to feel very ill. He started chewing on some grass <u>too</u> get his energy back.

<u>"I guess it's not that simple" said the donkey.</u>

17   Which of these should replace <u>were</u>?

    Ⓐ   are

    Ⓑ   does

    Ⓒ   is

    Ⓓ   was

18   Which of these should replace <u>followwed</u>?

    Ⓐ   folowed

    Ⓑ   folowwed

    Ⓒ   followed

    Ⓓ   folloowed

19 Which of these should replace <u>eated</u>?

    Ⓐ   ate

    Ⓑ   ated

    Ⓒ   eat

    Ⓓ   eaten

20 Which of these should replace <u>too</u>?

    Ⓐ   to

    Ⓑ   tow

    Ⓒ   two

    Ⓓ   toe

21 Write the last sentence correctly by adding a comma. Write the correct sentence below.

_____

22 Which sentence from the first paragraph does not belong in the story?

    Ⓐ   *He asked the grasshopper how he made such a wonderful sound.*

    Ⓑ   *The grasshopper explained that he lived off the dew.*

    Ⓒ   *Not many people realize that grasshoppers can also fly.*

    Ⓓ   *The donkey decided that he was going to eat dew until he could sing.*

END OF PRACTICE SET

English Language Arts

Practice Set 12

Reading

Nonfiction Text

Instructions

This set has one passage for you to read. The passage is followed by questions.

Read each question carefully. For each multiple-choice question, fill in the circle for the correct answer. For other types of questions, follow the instructions given. Some of the questions require a written answer. Write your answer on the lines provided.

Roger Federer

Roger Federer is a famous tennis player. He was born in Switzerland in 1981. Some people believe that he is the best tennis player ever. He became the world number one in 2005. He kept this rank for 237 weeks in a row. That is a record! He won 16 Grand Slam titles. That is also a record!

Roger plays well on clay, grass, and hard courts. However, he plays best on grass courts.

Wimbledon is a tennis contest held in Great Britain. Roger has won it six times. In 2008, he tried to win it for the sixth time in a row. He made the final. He was defeated by Spanish player Rafael Nadal. It was a close match. It was tough on both players. It was also great to watch. Some people say that it was the best tennis match ever played. This match also started a long row between the two players.

In 2009, Nadal was having knee problems. He was not well enough to compete in Wimbledon. Federer won that year. In 2010, Nadal beat Roger in the Wimbledon final. The two have competed in eight Grand Slam finals together. Nadal has won six of these.

© Derek Holtham

In 2010, Roger lost his number one ranking. Nadal became world number one. At the start of 2011, Roger was ranked third in the world. He may come back and become number one again. To do this, he will need to beat Nadal.

1   Read this sentence from the passage.

This match also started a long row between the two players.

Which word means about the same as <u>row</u>?

Ⓐ   Game

Ⓑ   Chat

Ⓒ   Fight

Ⓓ   Problem

2   In paragraph 3, what does the word <u>defeated</u> mean?

Ⓐ   Beaten

Ⓑ   Watched

Ⓒ   Surprised

Ⓓ   Hurt

3   Where was Roger Federer born?

Ⓐ   Great Britain

Ⓑ   Switzerland

Ⓒ   Spain

Ⓓ   United States

4   What is the first paragraph mainly about?

    Ⓐ   Roger Federer's success

    Ⓑ   Roger Federer's family

    Ⓒ   Roger Federer's problems

    Ⓓ   Roger Federer's childhood

5   Which sentence below is best supported by information in the passage?

    Ⓐ   Nadal dislikes playing Roger Federer.

    Ⓑ   Nadal became a better player than Roger Federer.

    Ⓒ   Nadal looked up to Roger Federer when he was young.

    Ⓓ   Nadal plays better on clay than Roger Federer.

6   Choose **two** details from the passage that support your answer to Question 5. Write the details on the lines below.

Supporting Detail 1:

_____

_____

Supporting Detail 2:

_____

_____

7   Circle the details listed below that are facts. Then add **two** more facts from the passage to the list.

Roger Federer is the best tennis player ever.

Roger Federer was born in 1981.

Roger Federer was number one for 237 weeks in a row.

Roger Federer is a great player to watch.

_____

_____

8   Why didn't Nadal compete in Wimbledon in 2009?

Ⓐ   He was too young.

Ⓑ   He had knee problems.

Ⓒ   He wasn't good enough.

Ⓓ   He had won too many times.

9   How did Roger most likely feel when he lost the 2008 Wimbledon final?

Ⓐ   Calm

Ⓑ   Upset

Ⓒ   Proud

Ⓓ   Scared

10   Read this sentence from the passage.

        It was a close match.

In which sentence does the word <u>close</u> mean the same as in the sentence above?

    Ⓐ   Kerry tried to <u>close</u> the door quietly.

    Ⓑ   They had to <u>close</u> off the street for the parade.

    Ⓒ   Joanne and Kendra are <u>close</u> friends.

    Ⓓ   James raced past Jonah and won the <u>close</u> race.

11   The author describes a 2008 Wimbledon final between Rafael Nadal and Roger Federer. Describe **two** reasons this match was important. Use information from the passage to support your answer.

_____

_____

_____

_____

_____

_____

_____

12 How does the author show that Roger Federer is a successful tennis player? Use at least **three** details from the passage in your answer.

_____

_____

_____

_____

_____

_____

_____

_____

_____

_____

_____

_____

_____

END OF PRACTICE SET

_____

English Language Arts

Practice Set 13

Reading

Literature Text

Instructions

This set has one passage for you to read. The passage is followed by questions.

Read each question carefully. For each multiple-choice question, fill in the circle for the correct answer. For other types of questions, follow the instructions given. Some of the questions require a written answer. Write your answer on the lines provided.

A Bold Decision

Steven loved playing for his basketball team. He had been playing basketball for as long as he could remember. Last year, they had won the state finals. This year, they were finding things much harder. There were only three games left in the season. Steven's team needed to win them all if they were going to the state playoffs. It was near the end of the game. They were behind by six points. Steven had just saved a basket with a great block. But he had hurt his knee as he landed.

"Are you okay to play?" asked his coach.

Steven frowned at the pain in his knee.

"I'll be fine," he said.

Steven knew the risks of his decision. He could risk hurting his knee even more. Or he could choose not to play. He knew that not playing might cause his team to lose. As he rested before the final quarter, he decided to play through the pain. He was going to win this game for the team he loved.

As the quarter started, he caught the ball after the other team made a mistake. He bounced the ball down the court and threw the ball into the hoop. Steven smiled towards his coach on the sidelines. They were only four points behind now.

Steven kept playing well during the final quarter. He even scored a three point shot from the center of the court. With just two minutes left on the clock, Steven's team was only one point behind. Steven was passed the ball by his teammate. He ignored the pain in his knee and sprinted forward. He headed towards the end of the court. His feet left the ground. He sent his shot into the basket and earned his side two points. The final whistle blew seconds after. Steven's bold decision had won his team the game.

1 In the sentence below, which word could best be used in place of <u>center</u>?

He even scored a three point shot from the center of the court.

ⓐ Edge

ⓑ Middle

ⓒ Back

ⓓ Front

2 Circle the **two** words from the passage that have about the same meaning.

finals   games   rested

decision   threw   choice

3 Which pair of sentences from the first paragraph best tell why the game is important to Steven? Tick **one** box below to show your choice.

☐ Steven loved playing for his basketball team. He had been playing basketball for as long as he could remember.

☐ Last year, they had won the state finals. This year, they were finding things much harder.

☐ There were only three games left in the season. Steven's team needed to win them all if they were going to the state playoffs.

☐ It was near the end of the game. They were behind by six points.

☐ Steven had just saved a basket with a great block. But he had hurt his knee as he landed.

4 What is Steven's bold decision?

   Ⓐ   Deciding to play when he is hurt

   Ⓑ   Deciding to take the final shot

   Ⓒ   Deciding to win the game

   Ⓓ   Deciding to try to make a three point shot

5 Read this sentence from the passage.

He ignored the pain in his knee and sprinted forward.

The word <u>sprinted</u> shows that Steven moved –

   Ⓐ   quickly

   Ⓑ   shakily

   Ⓒ   quietly

   Ⓓ   slowly

6 Why does Steven decide to play?

   Ⓐ   He really wants his team to win.

   Ⓑ   He does not want to upset his coach.

   Ⓒ   He does not realize that he is hurt.

   Ⓓ   He wants everyone to cheer for him.

7   What is the last paragraph mainly about?

    Ⓐ   How Steven's team won the game

    Ⓑ   How Steven felt at the end of the game

    Ⓒ   Why the game was important to Steven

    Ⓓ   How to shoot a basket correctly

8   Based on your answer to Question 7, explain why the last paragraph is important to the main idea of the story.

_____

_____

_____

_____

_____

_____

9   The author would probably describe Steven as –

    Ⓐ   kind

    Ⓑ   clever

    Ⓒ   silly

    Ⓓ   brave

10 Do you think Steven's team would have won if he had not of finished the game? Give at least **two** details from the passage to support your answer.

_____

_____

_____

_____

_____

11 Read this paragraph from the passage.

> **Steven knew the risks of his decision. He could risk hurting his knee even more. Or he could choose not to play. He knew that not playing might cause his team to lose. As he rested before the final quarter, he decided to play through the pain. He was going to win this game for the team he loved.**

What do you learn about Steven from this paragraph?

_____

_____

_____

_____

_____

12   In the passage, Steven makes a decision for the good of his team. Do you think that Steven did the right thing by deciding to keep playing? Explain why you feel that way.

_____

_____

_____

_____

_____

_____

_____

_____

_____

_____

_____

_____

END OF PRACTICE SET

English Language Arts

Practice Set 14

Reading and Writing

Nonfiction Text with Persuasive Writing Task

Instructions

This set has one passage for you to read. The passage is followed by questions.

Read each question carefully. For each multiple-choice question, fill in the circle for the correct answer. For other types of questions, follow the instructions given. Some of the questions require a written answer. Write your answer on the lines provided.

Rice Crispy Cakes

Rice crispy cakes are popular treats for children. Everybody loves how crunchy they are. The rice crispy and chocolate flavor is always a hit. And they are a perfect treat for sharing with friends. They are quick and easy to make too.

You only need a few simple things to make them. You will need some crispy rice cereal, butter, and a block of milk chocolate. You will also require a small bowl, a medium saucepan, a large saucepan, a baking tray, and patty cake holders.

What to Do

1. Start by pouring the crispy rice cereal into the small bowl.

2. Add 3 to 4 tablespoons of butter. It is a good idea to soften the butter first. Mix everything together with your hands. Just make sure you clean your hands first! You don't want to get dirt or germs through the mix.

3. You should now be able to fill the patty cake holders. Put a clump of the rice cereal mixture into each holder.

4. Next, you need to melt your block of chocolate. Fill a medium saucepan with water. Chop up about 2 ounces of chocolate. Place it in a small saucepan. Place the small saucepan in the medium saucepan. This will allow the hot water to gradually melt the bar of chocolate. Be careful you don't get water in with the chocolate. It will make the chocolate go hard and grainy. When your chocolate has turned to a thick liquid, it is ready to add to your crispy rice mixture.

5. Let the chocolate cool just enough so it does not burn you. Carefully pour a small amount of melted chocolate onto each ball of crispy rice. Make sure that each rice crispy cake is covered.

6. Arrange each crispy cake on the baking tray and place in the oven.

7. Bake them at 350 degrees for about 30 minutes.

8. When they're done baking, take them out of the oven and allow them to cool.

That's it! Your delicious treats are ready to enjoy or share!

****

1   In the sentence below, what does the word <u>gradually</u> most likely mean?

   This will allow the hot water to gradually melt the bar of chocolate.

  Ⓐ Nicely

  Ⓑ Slowly

  Ⓒ Firmly

  Ⓓ Quickly

2   Read these sentences from the passage.

   You will need some crispy rice cereal, butter, and a block of milk chocolate. You will also require a small bowl, a medium saucepan, a large saucepan, a baking tray, and patty cake holders.

  What would the author be best to use to give this information more clearly?

  Ⓐ Map

  Ⓑ List

  Ⓒ Diagram

  Ⓓ Timeline

3   What is probably the main purpose of softening the butter?

Ⓐ   To make it easier to mix with the cereal

Ⓑ   To help the chocolate melt

Ⓒ   To make the rice crispy cake cook quicker

Ⓓ   To make it easier to measure out

4   What is the main purpose of the passage?

Ⓐ   To teach readers how to do something

Ⓑ   To entertain readers with a story

Ⓒ   To inform readers about crispy rice cereal

Ⓓ   To compare different types of sweets

5   In Step 3, what does the word <u>clump</u> show?

Ⓐ   Only a small amount of mixture should be used.

Ⓑ   The mixture does not have to be a perfect shape.

Ⓒ   The mixture is made of rice crispy cereal.

Ⓓ   The mixture should be a smooth round ball.

6   When are the patty cake holders first needed? Circle the correct step.

Step 1   Step 2   Step 3   Step 4

Step 5   Step 6   Step 7   Step 8

7   Which of these would most help the reader make the rice crispy cakes?

Ⓐ   A picture of a box of cereal

Ⓑ   A list of different types of cereals

Ⓒ   A photograph of a rice crispy cake

Ⓓ   A timeline of the events

8   Which step does the photograph most help the reader complete?

Ⓐ   Step 3

Ⓑ   Step 4

Ⓒ   Step 5

Ⓓ   Step 6

9   What type of passage is "Rice Crispy Cakes"?

Ⓐ   Recipe

Ⓑ   Essay

Ⓒ   Advertisement

Ⓓ   Letter

10 Think about your answer to Question 9. Describe **two** features of the passage that help show what type it is.

Feature 1:

_____

_____

Feature 2:

_____

_____

11 Choose **two** more reasons the author gives to show that rice crispy cakes are a good treat to make. Write the details in the chart below.

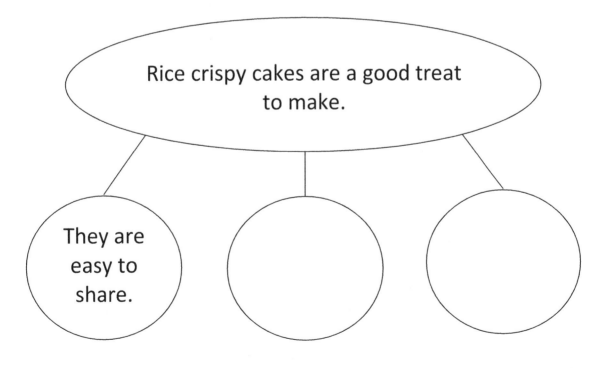

12   Choose **three** tasks to be done when making the rice crispy cakes where you would have to be careful. Explain why you have to be careful and what you should do to stop things going wrong. Use information from the passage to support your answer.

_____

_____

_____

_____

_____

_____

_____

_____

_____

_____

_____

_____

_____

13 The passage describes something that young people can cook. Do you think it's important that young people learn to cook? Write an opinion article that tells your opinion and explains why you feel that way. In your article, include **three** reasons to support your opinion.

_____

_____

_____

_____

_____

_____

_____

_____

_____

_____

_____

_____

_____

_____

_____

END OF PRACTICE SET

English Language Arts

Practice Set 15

Reading and Writing

Nonfiction Text with Informative Writing Task

Instructions

This set has one passage for you to read. The passage is followed by questions.

Read each question carefully. For each multiple-choice question, fill in the circle for the correct answer. For other types of questions, follow the instructions given. Some of the questions require a written answer. Write your answer on the lines provided.

The New York Times

The New York Times is an American newspaper. It was founded in New York. It was first printed in 1851. The first issue cost just 1 cent to buy. It is printed each day. Each issue is read by around one million people. The newspaper has won over 110 Pulitzer Prizes. A Pulitzer Prize is an award given for excellent reporting. This is more than any other newspaper or magazine.

The New York Times is the largest local newspaper in the United States. It is also the third largest newspaper overall. Only *The Wall Street Journal* and *USA Today* are read by more people.

Even though it is still popular, it sells fewer copies today than in the past. In 1990, it was read by over a million people. By 2010, it was being read by less than a million people. This change has occurred for most printed newspapers. The main reason is that people can read the news on the Internet for free.

The newspaper's motto is "All the News That's Fit to Print." This appears printed in the top corner of the front page.

The newspaper has many different sections. It covers news, business, and science. It also covers sport, home, and fashion. It has sections for travel, food, art, and movies. It is also known for its difficult crossword puzzles.

In 2011, each issue sold for $2. However, the Sunday issue is larger. It is sold for $5.

Hundreds of people work to create *The New York Times* every day.

1 Read this sentence from the passage.

It was founded in New York.

What does the word <u>founded</u> mean in the sentence?

Ⓐ   Sold

Ⓑ   Discovered

Ⓒ   Started

Ⓓ   Lost

2 Read this sentence from the passage.

The newspaper's motto is "All the News That's Fit to Print."

As it is used in this sentence, what does <u>fit</u> mean?

Ⓐ   Ready

Ⓑ   Healthy

Ⓒ   Right

Ⓓ   Known

3   According to the passage, how is *The Wall Street Journal* different from *The New York Times*?

Ⓐ   It is read by more people.

Ⓑ   It has won more awards.

Ⓒ   It costs less to buy.

Ⓓ   It has fewer sections.

4   According to the passage, why are fewer copies of *The New York Times* sold today than in the past?

Ⓐ   It costs too much.

Ⓑ   People read the news online.

Ⓒ   People buy other newspapers instead.

Ⓓ   It has too many sections.

5   Which word best describes the tone of the passage?

Ⓐ   Gloomy

Ⓑ   Serious

Ⓒ   Lively

Ⓓ   Hopeful

6   Which detail best shows that *The New York Times* is successful?

Ⓐ   It is printed seven days a week.

Ⓑ   Its price has increased to $2.

Ⓒ   It has a motto.

Ⓓ   It has won over 110 Pulitzer Prizes.

7   Use details from the passage to complete the web below.

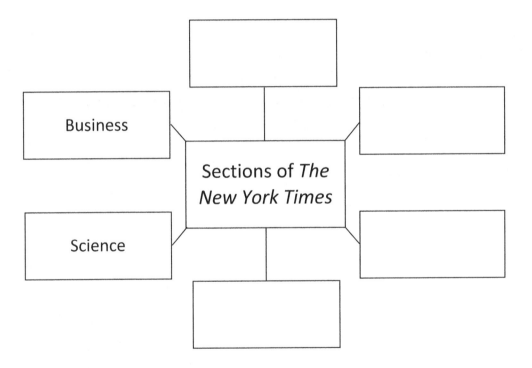

8   Read this sentence from the passage.

The main reason is that people can read the news on the Internet for free.

In which sentence does <u>free</u> mean the same as in the sentence above?

Ⓐ   Jorja gave the kitten away for <u>free</u>.

Ⓑ   Andy was happy to have the whole day <u>free</u>.

Ⓒ   The diner was so busy that only one table was <u>free</u>.

Ⓓ   The beach always made Kyle feel relaxed and <u>free</u>.

9   Read this sentence from the passage.

The newspaper has won over 110 Pulitzer Prizes. A Pulitzer Prize is an award given for excellent reporting.

Explain why the second sentence is important. In your answer, explain what the second sentence tells you about *The New York Times*.

_____

_____

_____

_____

_____

_____

10   Describe **two** things about *The New York Times* that have changed since it was first printed.

1: _____

_____

2: _____

_____

11   Which details from the passage did you find most interesting? Explain why you found those details interesting. Use details from the passage in your answer.

_____

_____

_____

_____

_____

_____

12 The passage describes how many people today read the news on the Internet. Explain why you think people choose to read the news online. Explain how this trend is likely to affect newspapers like *The New York Times*.

In your response, be sure to
- explain why you think people choose to read the news online
- describe at least two benefits of reading the news online
- explain how people reading the news online will affect newspapers like *The New York Times*
- use details from the passage to support your answer

_____

_____

_____

_____

_____

_____

_____

_____

_____

_____

_____

_____

_____

_____

_____

_____

_____

_____

_____

_____

_____

_____

_____

_____

_____

_____

_____

_____

_____

END OF PRACTICE SET

English Language Arts

Practice Set 16

Reading and Writing

Literature Text with Narrative Writing Task

Instructions

This set has one passage for you to read. The passage is followed by questions.

Read each question carefully. For each multiple-choice question, fill in the circle for the correct answer. For other types of questions, follow the instructions given. Some of the questions require a written answer. Write your answer on the lines provided.

Little Things
by Ebenezer Cobham Brewer

Little drops of water,
Little grains of sand,
Make the mighty ocean
And the pleasant land.

Thus the little minutes,
Humble though they be,
Make the mighty ages
Of eternity.

This canyon in Arizona is a popular place for tourists and adventure-seekers. People love to admire the view, take photographs, or raft along the Colorado River. It took millions of years for the canyon to form. As water flowed over the land, it wore away the rock little by little. Today, the result is a canyon that is thousands of feet deep.

1   In the lines below, what does the word <u>eternity</u> most likely mean?

Make the mighty ages
Of eternity.

Ⓐ   Time

Ⓑ   Forever

Ⓒ   Earth

Ⓓ   Everything

2   Read this line from the poem.

Make the mighty ocean

The word <u>mighty</u> suggests that the ocean is –

Ⓐ   strange

Ⓑ   scary

Ⓒ   powerful

Ⓓ   small

3   How many stanzas does the poem have? Circle the correct answer.

1   2   3   4   5   6   7   8

4   Which literary technique does the author use in the line below?

   Make the mighty ages

   Ⓐ   Alliteration

   Ⓑ   Simile

   Ⓒ   Metaphor

   Ⓓ   Flashback

5   What is the rhyme pattern of each stanza of the poem?

   Ⓐ   All the lines rhyme with each other.

   Ⓑ   There are two pairs of rhyming lines.

   Ⓒ   The second and fourth lines rhyme.

   Ⓓ   None of the lines rhyme.

6   What are the lines below mainly about?

   Thus the little minutes,
   Humble though they be,
   Make the mighty ages
   Of eternity.

   Ⓐ   Nature

   Ⓑ   Earth

   Ⓒ   Time

   Ⓓ   Sleep

7   What is the main idea of the poem?

    Ⓐ   Little things can form great things.

    Ⓑ   Everything is always changing.

    Ⓒ   Life could not survive without water.

    Ⓓ   Time can go fast or slow.

8   Circle **all** the words that are repeated in the poem.

little   drops   mighty

water   sand   minutes

9   Explain how water, sand, and minutes are similar in the poem. Use details from the poem to support your answer.

_____

_____

_____

_____

_____

_____

10   Look at the picture of the canyon and read the caption. What idea does this show that is also a main idea in the poem?

_____

_____

_____

_____

_____

_____

11   Based on your answer to Question 10, choose **two** details given in the caption that best show the main idea.

1: _____

_____

2: _____

_____

12 Just like how small grains of sand can create a large desert, small actions can create larger things over time. Think of an example from your life of how your small actions have led to something bigger over time. Describe what small actions you took and what they led to.

In your response, be sure to
- describe a time when small actions led to something bigger
- describe the small actions you took
- describe what happened because of the small actions you took

_____

_____

_____

_____

_____

_____

_____

_____

_____

_____

_____

_____

_____

_____

_____

_____

_____

_____

_____

_____

_____

_____

_____

_____

_____

_____

END OF PRACTICE SET

English Language Arts

Practice Set 17

Reading

Nonfiction Text

Instructions

This set has one passage for you to read. The passage is followed by questions.

Read each question carefully. For each multiple-choice question, fill in the circle for the correct answer. For other types of questions, follow the instructions given. Some of the questions require a written answer. Write your answer on the lines provided.

The Shining Light Day Center

 As parents, the wellbeing of your children is very important. It is important to keep them happy and healthy. It is also important to make sure their bodies and minds are active. It is especially important for children under the age of five. During this time, children can learn good fitness habits that they will keep for life.

During this time, children also learn quickly. They are at a special age where they take in information quickly. They also develop skills easier. It is important to find time to develop both their bodies and minds.

As parents, it can be hard to find time for all this. At the Shining Light Day Center, we understand this. We have created a range of activities to help your child.

Our activities cover many different areas. We want to help children think and learn. We want to help children learn to work with others. We want to help children learn to read and speak. We also want to help children be fit and healthy. Our activities include classes, games, and time for free play. These keep the child interested. At the same time, they are learning and growing.

Our programs are aimed at children between the ages of 3 and 5. Children will enjoy playing with others. They will learn basic math and English skills. Our program helps children start grade school. Think of it as a head start for your child!

Our classes are held at two different times. On weekdays, classes are held from noon to 3 p.m. On weekends, classes are held from 9 to 11 a.m. This gives you a lot of choice as a parent. You can choose the day and time that best suits you.

All parents should consider the Shining Light Day Center. It will give your child the best head start in life. Visit our website today to learn more. You can also call a member of our staff to discuss your child's future. You can also drop in any time to watch a class.

Learning Activity	Details
Storytelling	Children listen to stories being told. They answer questions about the story. Then they help write the ending to the story.
Telling Time	Students learn counting skills by using clocks. They count hours and minutes.
Hide and Seek	Children must find blocks hidden in our outdoor play areas. They race to find all the blocks of their color.
Puppet Show	Children use hand puppets to act out stories. They work in pairs.

1   Read this sentence from the passage.

        They also develop skills easier.

    Which word means the opposite of <u>easier</u>?

    Ⓐ   Simpler

    Ⓑ   Harder

    Ⓒ   Quicker

    Ⓓ   Slower

2   Which two words from the passage have about the same meaning?

    Ⓐ   *read, speak*

    Ⓑ   *fit, healthy*

    Ⓒ   *day, time*

    Ⓓ   *learning, school*

3   The passage is most like –

    Ⓐ   an essay

    Ⓑ   an advertisement

    Ⓒ   a short story

    Ⓓ   a news article

4 How is the third paragraph mainly organized?

    Ⓐ A problem is described and then a solution is given.

    Ⓑ Events are described in the order they occur.

    Ⓒ Facts are given to support an argument.

    Ⓓ A question is asked and then answered.

5 Read this sentence from the passage.

You can also drop in any time to watch a class.

What do the words "drop in" mean?

    Ⓐ Phone

    Ⓑ Check

    Ⓒ Visit

    Ⓓ Watch

6 The passage was probably written mainly to –

    Ⓐ encourage parents to send their children to the day center

    Ⓑ compare the day center with grade school

    Ⓒ describe why the day center was started

    Ⓓ inform parents about the benefits of learning

7 The web below describes the different areas covered by the activities. Complete the chart by listing **two** more areas covered by the activities.

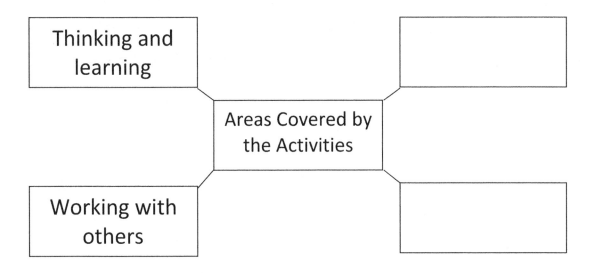

8 What do you think the author's main purpose for including the table is? Use details from the passage in your answer.

_____

_____

_____

_____

_____

_____

9   Which sentence is included mainly to persuade the reader?

Ⓐ   *As parents, it can be hard to find time for all this.*

Ⓑ   *Our programs are aimed at children between the ages of 3 and 5.*

Ⓒ   *On weekdays, classes are held from noon to 3 p.m.*

Ⓓ   *It will give your child the best head start in life.*

10   Which activity from the table would be most likely to develop math skills?

Ⓐ   Storytelling

Ⓑ   Telling Time

Ⓒ   Hide and Seek

Ⓓ   Puppet Show

11   Read these sentences from the first paragraph.

> **It is also important to make sure their bodies and minds are active.**
> **It is especially important for children under the age of five.**

List **two** reasons the author gives to show why it is important for children under the age of five.

1: _____

_____

2: _____

_____

12 The passage describes many benefits of sending children to the Shining Light Day Center. Describe at least **three** benefits to children of going to the Shining Light Day Center. Use details from the passage in your answer.

_____

_____

_____

_____

_____

_____

_____

_____

_____

_____

_____

_____

_____

END OF PRACTICE SET

English Language Arts

Practice Set 18

Reading and Writing

Paired Literature Texts with Writing Task

Instructions

This set has two short passages for you to read. Read each passage and answer the questions that follow it.

For each multiple-choice question, fill in the circle for the correct answer. For other types of questions, follow the instructions given. Some of the questions require a written answer. Write your answer on the lines provided.

After reading both passages, you will use information from both passages to answer a question. Write your answer on the lines provided.

Vacation Time

Quinn, Harley, and Max were sitting beside the basketball court eating lunch.

"What are you doing this summer, Harley?" Quinn asked.

"Well, I'll probably go to see my grandparents in Florida," Harley replied. "What about you?"

"That sounds like fun. I'm probably going to go visit my Dad in Australia!" Quinn said.

"What about you?" Quinn asked Max.

"I'm going to stay here in town," Max said.

Quinn and Harley both shook their heads sadly.

"Well, that sounds awfully boring," Harley said.

Max tilted his head a little and thought for a moment.

"Well, I'm going to watch television, play basketball, go to the local swimming pool, ride my bike, play computer games, read some books..."

Max went on and on and listed even more things he was going to do.

Quinn stared at Max, "Oh boy, is that all?"

The boys laughed and ate the rest of their lunch.

1   Which statement is most likely true about Max?

    Ⓐ   He wishes he could visit Australia.

    Ⓑ   He is looking forward to summer.

    Ⓒ   He thinks summer will be boring.

    Ⓓ   He wants his friends to stay in town.

2   What is the passage mainly about?

    Ⓐ   Three boys discussing their vacations

    Ⓑ   Three boys trying to think of something fun to do

    Ⓒ   Three boys playing basketball together

    Ⓓ   Three boys arguing about what to do together

3   In which sentence from the passage is the character being humorous?

    Ⓐ   *"What are you doing this summer, Harley?" Quinn asked.*

    Ⓑ   *"I'm going to stay here in town," Max said.*

    Ⓒ   *"Well, that sounds awfully boring," Harley said.*

    Ⓓ   *Quinn stared at Max, "Oh boy, is that all?"*

4   What does the photograph in the passage represent?

    Ⓐ   What Quinn and Harley will miss most when they are away

    Ⓑ   Where the boys are talking about their summers

    Ⓒ   How you can do fun things on your own

    Ⓓ   One of the things Max plans to do over summer

5   How are Max's vacation plans different from Quinn's and Hoy's? Use details from the passage in your answer.

_____

_____

_____

_____

_____

6   Do you think that Max's vacation plans sound interesting or dull? Use details from the passage in your answer.

_____

_____

_____

_____

_____

Fish Food

"Come on, it's not that far now!" Sam yelled.

Ben wiped away some sweat and kept going. It was a very warm day, and it just kept getting warmer.

Sam and Ben were on their way to the big lake to catch some fish. They had their fishing rods and some bait to put on their hooks.

They finally found a good spot near the lake. They sat down to start fishing. Ben opened the ice cream container where he had asked his mother to put the bait.

"This is not fishing bait. These worms are made of candy!" Ben said. "I should have told Mom I wanted worms to use as bait."

"We could still try," Sam offered. "Maybe the fish will like the candy worms."

Ben wasn't sure it would work, but it sounded like fun. He didn't mind if they didn't catch anything anyway. He just liked sitting back and enjoying a lazy afternoon by the lake.

"It's worth a try," Ben said. "But we should keep a few worms for ourselves."

7   What will Sam and Ben most likely do next?

(A)   Start eating the candy worms

(B)   Start fishing using the candy worms

(C)   Choose a different spot to fish

(D)   Decide to go home and do something else

8   What is the most likely reason Ben's mother put candy in the ice cream container?

(A)   She thought that they would make good bait.

(B)   She didn't realize that Ben wanted worms for bait.

(C)   She didn't want Sam and Ben to catch any fish.

(D)   She wanted Sam and Ben to have a snack to eat.

9   What happens right after Ben opens the ice cream container?

(A)   He sees that he has candy worms.

(B)   He finds a good fishing spot.

(C)   He decides to fish anyway.

(D)   He asks his mother to pack the bait.

10   The photograph in the passage mainly makes the lake seem like –

(A)   a busy place

(B)   an exciting place

(C)   a peaceful place

(D)   a lonely place

11   The setting of a story is where and when it takes place. Complete the table below by stating what you think the setting is in the second column. In the last column, describe the detail from the story that helped you decide what the setting was.

	Setting	Supporting Details
Where the story takes place		
What time of day the story takes place		
What time of year the story takes place		

12 Max and Sam can both be described as characters that make the most out of things. Explain how you can tell that Max and Sam both like to make the most out of things. Use details from both passages in your answer.

_____

_____

_____

_____

_____

_____

_____

_____

_____

_____

END OF PRACTICE SET

English Language Arts

Practice Set 19

Writing

Research, Writing Process, and Writing Conventions

Instructions

The first four questions in this set are writing or research tasks. Read the information and then answer the questions.

This set also has short passages that contain errors or opportunities for improvement. Read each passage and answer the questions that follow it. For each multiple-choice question, fill in the circle for the correct answer. For other types of questions, follow the instructions given.

A student is writing a research paper for history class about Pennsylvania. Read the source below. Then answer the following two questions.

King Charles the Second of England owed a large sum of money to a young Englishman named William Penn. The king had spent so much money that he had none left to pay his debts. Penn knew this, so he told the king that if he would give him a piece of wild land in America, he would ask nothing more.

Charles was very glad to settle the account so easily. He gave Penn a great territory north of Maryland and west of the Delaware River. The king named it Pennsylvania, a word which means Penn's Woods. At that time the land was not thought to be worth much. No one then had discovered the fact that beneath Penn's Woods there were huge amounts of coal and iron, which would one day be of greater value than all the riches of the king of England.

1   The student wants to write a paragraph about how King Charles made an error when giving the land away. Circle **two** sentences from the source that could be used to support this idea.

2   Write a short paragraph that tells about King Charles's error. Use details from the sentences you circled in the paragraph.

_____

_____

_____

_____

_____

A student is writing an opinion article about trying new things. Read the plan for the opinion article. Then answer the following two questions.

Claim: You should keep trying new things.
Supporting idea: You won't find out what you're good at unless you try it.
Supporting idea: You will learn new skills.
Supporting idea: It's good to challenge yourself.

3   Write one or two sentences that could be used to start the article. The sentences should state the main claim of the article.

_____

_____

_____

4   Choose one of the supporting ideas listed. Write a paragraph that uses the supporting idea to show that you should keep trying new things.

_____

_____

_____

_____

_____

The passage below contains errors. The words or phrases that are incorrect are underlined. For each word or phrase underlined, answer the question below.

a day of learning

It's a Saturday and that means no school. I decided to feed my brain for the day. This morning I <u>did start</u> reading through an encyclopedia. They <u>will have</u> always amazed me with how much information is in them. I enjoyed reading about Scotland, badgers, and a writer named Aldous Huxley. I also read all about the first President of the United States, George Washington. It might sound like a <u>boreing</u> day to some people, <u>so</u> I actually had a great time! I learned a lot of new things and I want to learn even <u>moor</u>.

5   What is the correct way to capitalize the title? Write your answer below.

_____

6   Which of these should replace <u>did start</u>?

    Ⓐ   start

    Ⓑ   starts

    Ⓒ   started

    Ⓓ   starting

7 Which of these should replace <u>will have</u>?

Ⓐ had

Ⓑ have

Ⓒ did have

Ⓓ will have

8 Which of these should replace <u>boreing</u>?

Ⓐ boring

Ⓑ borring

Ⓒ booring

Ⓓ boorring

9 Which of these should replace <u>so</u>?

Ⓐ and

Ⓑ but

Ⓒ if

Ⓓ then

10 As it is used in the sentence, what is the correct spelling of <u>moor</u>? Write your answer below.

_____

The passage below contains errors. The words or phrases that are incorrect are underlined. For each word or phrase underlined, answer the question below.

Volcanoes

Hot magma and gases build up inside the earth's crust. Every now and then, it <u>bersts</u> out from under the surface. The result is a volcano. When a volcano blows, rocks and ash can be <u>throwed</u> out high into the atmosphere. Quite <u>amazing</u>, it can reach many miles high.

A volcano forms when <u>their</u> is magma under the surface. Magma is melted rock <u>beneeth</u> the earth's surface. When the magma is above the earth's surface, it is called lava. If you touched lava with a steel rod, the steel rod would melt in seconds. It's hard to imagine, <u>so</u> that's how hot lava is.

11   What is the correct way to spell <u>bersts</u>? Write your answer below.

_____

12   Which of these should replace <u>throwed</u>?

Ⓐ   threw

Ⓑ   throw

Ⓒ   thrown

Ⓓ   throwing

13 Which of these should replace <u>amazing</u>?

Ⓐ   amaze

Ⓑ   amazed

Ⓒ   amazingly

Ⓓ   amazement

14 As it is used in the sentence, what is the correct spelling of <u>their</u>? Write your answer below.

_____

15 Which of these should replace <u>beneeth</u>?

Ⓐ   beneith

Ⓑ   benieth

Ⓒ   benaeth

Ⓓ   beneath

16 Which of these should replace <u>so</u>?

Ⓐ   and

Ⓑ   but

Ⓒ   for

Ⓓ   or

The passage below contains errors. The words or phrases that are incorrect are underlined. For each word or phrase underlined, answer the question below.

Stewart the Dragon

Stewart was a <u>very big, green, dragon</u>. He lived in a cave on the top of a hill. The people in the town below were very scared of him. If they ever <u>sore</u> Stewart, they ran inside to hide. This made Stewart very sad. He did not want to hert anybody. He just wanted to be part of the town. It always looked like everyone was having lots of fun.

One night it <u>were</u> very cold, and the people of the town could not start the fire. Stewart went down to the town. He used his fire breath to start the fire. The people of the town realized that Stewart was a helpful and <u>careing</u> dragon. They invited Stewart to come down to the town every night. Stewart started the fire each night. Then he ate and <u>drinked</u> with the villagers, before returning <u>happly</u> to his home.

17   Which of these should replace <u>very big, green, dragon</u>?

    Ⓐ   very big green dragon

    Ⓑ   very big, green dragon

    Ⓒ   very big green, dragon

    Ⓓ   very, big green dragon

18   As it is used in the sentence, what is the correct spelling of <u>sore</u>? Write your answer below.

_____

19   Which of these should replace <u>were</u>?

Ⓐ   are

Ⓑ   be

Ⓒ   is

Ⓓ   was

20   Which of these should replace <u>careing</u>?

Ⓐ   caring

Ⓑ   carring

Ⓒ   cearing

Ⓓ   cearring

21   Which of these should replace <u>drinked</u>?

Ⓐ   drank

Ⓑ   drink

Ⓒ   drinking

Ⓓ   dranked

22   Which of these should replace <u>happly</u>?

Ⓐ   hapilly

Ⓑ   happilly

Ⓒ   happily

Ⓓ   hapily

END OF PRACTICE SET

English Language Arts

Practice Set 20

Reading and Writing

Paired Nonfiction Texts with Writing Task

Instructions

This set has two short passages for you to read. Read each passage and answer the questions that follow it.

For each multiple-choice question, fill in the circle for the correct answer. For other types of questions, follow the instructions given. Some of the questions require a written answer. Write your answer on the lines provided.

After reading both passages, you will use information from both passages to answer a question. Write your answer on the lines provided.

Nintendo

Did you know that Nintendo didn't always make video game consoles? Before the first Nintendo gaming console was ever thought of, Nintendo was making playing cards!

Nintendo was originally founded in 1889 to make playing cards for a game called Hanafuda. Nintendo later tried many different business ideas before finding its success. These included a taxi company, a television network, and a food company.

All of Nintendo's earlier business attempts eventually failed. It was not until 1983 when Nintendo launched the original Nintendo Entertainment System (NES) that the company found commercial success. A handheld game console called the Game Boy followed in 1989.

It has since gone on to make other similar products. The Nintendo DS was released in 2004 and has sold over 150 million units. The Nintendo Wii was launched in 2006. It was a gaming system that was able to sense the movements of players, and use the physical movements of the player to direct the game. For example, someone playing tennis would swing the controller to cause the player in the game to swing the tennis racket. The Wii sold over 90 million units in less than 5 years.

The Nintendo DS and the Nintendo Wii changed the future of the company.

1   The passage states that Nintendo did not find commercial success until 1983. Which word could best be used in place of <u>commercial</u>?

    Ⓐ   Business

    Ⓑ   Long-term

    Ⓒ   Sudden

    Ⓓ   Public

2   Why does the author begin the passage with a question?

    Ⓐ   To show that the information may not be true

    Ⓑ   To get readers interested in the topic of the passage

    Ⓒ   To suggest that readers should research the topic

    Ⓓ   To explain how Nintendo changed over the years

3   If the passage was given another title, which title would best fit?

    Ⓐ   The Future of Nintendo

    Ⓑ   How to Play Nintendo

    Ⓒ   Collecting Playing Cards

    Ⓓ   The Beginnings of a Business

4   The photographs are most likely included in the passage to –

    Ⓐ   provide examples of Nintendo's successful products

    Ⓑ   help readers understand what made Nintendo's products successful

    Ⓒ   demonstrate how important it was that Nintendo did not give up

    Ⓓ   show how the Nintendo Wii was different from other systems

5 Complete the web below using information from the passage.

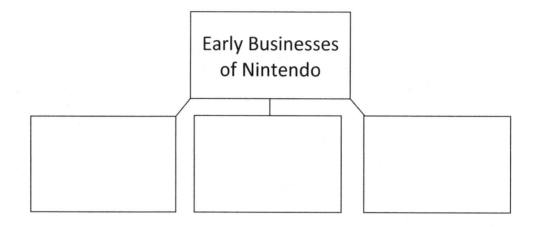

6 List the entertainment products created by Nintendo in the order they were created.

_____

_____

_____

_____

_____

_____

Breaking In

Today, Apple is a success in the personal computer market. It offers a range of effective and attractive products. But it wasn't always that way. Apple had to struggle to break into the market.

At the time, IBM was the leader in the market. Most people wanted to buy IBM computers, and very few wanted the Apple products. Then Apple introduced the iMac G3 in 1998. The iMac G3 was one of the first real successes for Apple. Previous to the iMac, Apple saw only limited success with its earlier desktop models.

The iMac G3 came after new Apple CEO Steve Jobs decided to trim Apple's product line. He decided to focus on making products that people would like. It was a bold move and an effective one. The striking design of the iMac was just one of the reasons it was special.

The iMac G3 was unlike any computer that had been seen. The computer parts were no longer in a separate case, but were part of the monitor. The computer now looked better and took up less space. It was first released in blue, but other bright colors were soon added. The color and style were an immediate hit. Unlike the drab computers others offered, the iMac looked bright and fun to use.

7   Read this sentence from the passage.

> **The iMac G3 came after new Apple CEO Steve Jobs decided to trim Apple's product line.**

The word <u>trim</u> is used to show that Steve Jobs –

Ⓐ   made each product smaller

Ⓑ   reduced the number of products

Ⓒ   decreased the weight of the products

Ⓓ   made the products look more attractive

8   The author probably wrote this passage to –

Ⓐ   encourage people to buy Apple products

Ⓑ   describe a turning point for a company

Ⓒ   analyze the sales methods of a computer company

Ⓓ   tell about the life of Steve Jobs

9   Which sentence from the passage is a fact?

Ⓐ   *It offers a range of effective and attractive products.*

Ⓑ   *Then Apple introduced the iMac G3 in 1998.*

Ⓒ   *It was a bold move and an effective one.*

Ⓓ   *The striking design of the iMac was just one of the reasons it was special.*

10   Complete the table below by describing **two** ways the iMac G3 was different from other computers at the time.

Other Computers at the Time	The iMac G3

11   Read this sentence from the passage.

He decided to focus on making products that people would like.

Did the iMac G3 achieve this? Use details from the passage and the caption to support your answer.

_____

_____

_____

_____

_____

_____

12 Think about what you learned about the companies Nintendo and Apple. Describe how their histories are similar and how they are different. Use details from both passages in your answer.

In your response, be sure to
- describe how the histories of Nintendo and Apple are similar
- describe how the histories of Nintendo and Apple are different
- use details from both passages to support your answer

_____

_____

_____

_____

_____

_____

_____

_____

_____

_____

_____

_____

END OF PRACTICE SET

English Language Arts

Practice Set 21

Research and Writing

Persuasive Writing Task

Instructions
Read the passages that follow.
Then read the writing prompt and complete the writing task.

Source 1: Sleep Well, Live Well
by Anderson Lucas

I have noticed that many students are coming to school tired. I am worried about this because I think it will affect their happiness and learning. Many students have so much to do that they stay up late. It gives them time to fit in schoolwork, sports, hobbies, and time with friends. But if you do not get enough sleep, you might not do any of these things well.

When you sleep, you are preparing your brain for the next day. If you get enough sleep, you will be able to concentrate at school better and easily remember information. Studies have shown that a good night's sleep improves learning and creativity.

You need a good night's sleep for play as well. Whether you are playing an instrument or playing sport, you need to be well rested. If you don't get a good night's sleep, then you will not have the energy to fully participate. Also, your decision making and problem solving skills could suffer.

Sleep is also important for your emotional health. If you have a good night's sleep, it will be easier to control your emotions. You are more likely to feel happy and enjoy the day. If you are happy, you get along with everybody. You will feel motivated to be a good person and helps others.

Sleep is also important for your health and safety. Sleep allows your body to heal and can reduce the risk of certain diseases. If you are sick, sleep helps you to recover more quickly. It helps keep everything in your body in perfect balance. Also, if you sleep well you will be alert and react faster. This will help to prevent poor decisions. Poor decisions can put you and others at risk.

I have noticed that many students are not getting enough sleep. Please try to turn off the television, put down your phone, and go to bed earlier. If you get more sleep, you will learn better, play better, feel happier, and protect yourself and others. These are good reasons to get more sleep.

Source 2: Kids Want to Sleep In
by Noelle Zhang

I think that we should start school later in the day. My school starts at 8 o'clock in the morning, but I am very tired at this time. My mother wakes me up for school just past 6 o'clock, which is far too early. I hate getting out of bed so early in the morning. My two sisters don't like getting up either, and I'm sure there are many students who feel the same way.

I often try to go to bed at an earlier time, but I can't sleep. Sometimes I read my book with my flashlight at night. My mother tells me to turn off the light because I will be tired, but I want to stay awake and read. By the time I finally feel ready to sleep, it is very late. In the morning, I wake up feeling like I need a few more hours. I sleep in as long as I can, and then I rush to school. I often skip breakfast because I am in such a rush.

I often don't pay attention during the first class of the day because I am tired and hungry. I cannot think during class because I have not eaten breakfast. If school started later, there would be time for breakfast in the morning. There might even be time for some morning exercise. Then I would arrive at school feeling fresh and ready to learn.

I would be a lot happier if I started school two hours later. I think it would be better for everyone. I learned in science class that sleep is very important for the body. I learned that kids actually sleep more hours than adults. This is because kids are learning and growing. Students who get more sleep will be better learners. This will make the teachers happy because they will no longer be frustrated by tired students who are not listening.

I think everyone can agree that this is a good idea. Students can sleep more and can have time to eat breakfast. We can be more focused during class. Starting school later will be of great benefit to students, teachers, and parents.

Source 3: Sleep Poster
by Archer Lewis

Writing Prompt

Write an article for the school newspaper in which you argue that even though students today are very busy, they need to make time for a proper night's sleep. Use information from the passages in your article.

Be sure to include

- an introduction;
- support for your opinion using information from the passages; and
- a conclusion that is related to your opinion.

END OF PRACTICE SET

English Language Arts

Practice Set 22

Research and Writing

Informative Writing Task

Instructions
Read the passages that follow. Then read the writing prompt and complete the writing task.

Source 1: Mother Teresa
by Leonie Graham

Mother Teresa was a well-loved humanitarian of the 20th century. She was born in Albania on August 25, 1910. She died on September 5, 1997. Mother Teresa served the poor in India and in other countries. She is honored by many people and the Catholic Church for her service to the poor. She received the Nobel Peace Prize for her work in 1979 and became a saint in 2016.

Mother Teresa was born with the name Agnes Bojaxhiu. When she was a child, her mother taught her to always feed the poor. She went to an elementary school run by nuns. Mother Teresa went on a pilgrimage when she was 12. She wanted to become a nun. At 18, she joined the Sisters of Loreto in Dublin, Ireland. Later, she went with the sisters to India. She worked at a high school for poor girls in India. She taught history and geography. She also learned Hindi and Bengali in India. She made final vows to the Sisters of Loreto in 1937. She changed her name to Mother Teresa when she made final vows. In 1946, she wanted to leave the nuns to work with the poor every day. In 1948, the Pope gave her permission to leave the sisters.

She was determined to give poor people the opportunity to learn. She believed that this was the way for people to overcome poverty. She went to live in the poorest areas of India where she believed that people needed her the most. First, she opened an open-air school for poor students. When people saw the work that she was doing, they helped her. People gave money and time to help her. Mother Teresa opened an orphanage, a nursing home, and many clinics in India. She got many people to volunteer with her.

In 1971, she went to America. She opened a home for poor people in America. She also went to Beirut and Armenia to help people. She won many awards for the good things she did. Mother Teresa is thought of by many people as the greatest saint of all time.

Source 2: Jane Goodall – An Expert on Chimpanzees
by Damon Ryan

For over 50 years, Dr. Jane Goodall has studied animals and their environment. As a little girl, she observed native birds and animals. She loved to draw them and to make notes about what they did. She dreamed of traveling to Africa to see wild animals.

When she was 26, her wish came true. She traveled to Africa. She visited the countries of Kenya and Tanzania. She went to a national park in Tanzania for many years. She spent her time there studying chimpanzees. Chimpanzees are smaller monkeys covered with long black hair. They have a thick body with long arms, short legs, and no tail.

Every day she would go and observe the chimpanzees in their feeding area. She would always go at the same time. She would climb trees, copy their behavior, and eat the foods that they ate. After about two years, a chimpanzee came up to her. He did not show any fear. She named him David Greybeard. Soon he was taking bananas out of her hand. He even let her groom him. Other chimpanzees watched Dr. Goodall and David. This allowed Goodall to observe the monkeys closely.

She observed how they acted in families and how they got along with each other in the chimpanzee community. She was able to keep records on 50 different chimpanzees. That is about half of the chimpanzees in the park.

She learned many things. First, she learned that they made about 20 different sounds to communicate. They hoot, scream, and grunt. They drum on tree trunks with their hands. Each sound means something else. This is like our language where our tone of voice is used to communicate what we want to say. Each chimpanzee has a different hoot from the others. They also use their faces and bodies to communicate.

 She also saw that chimpanzees could make and use tools. For example, they would stick blades of grass and leaves into termite hills to try to get some of them to crawl out. This was the first time in history that animals other than humans were seen making tools.

In addition, she observed that chimpanzees shared emotions. They could comfort one another by hugging. They would touch each other often. They would kiss when they met. They held hands and groomed each other. She enjoyed watching the families. She was amazed that the mothers nursed and cared for their babies for five years before giving birth again.

Goodall thought all of these findings were very interesting. She found out that chimpanzees were very smart. In many ways, they were like human beings. She returned to England to study animal behavior at college.

After she finished school, it was time to return to Tanzania. She discovered more and more interesting things about chimpanzees. She gave names to each of the chimpanzees that she studied. In her journals, she recorded their behaviors and personalities. Before this time, scientists did not really know that much about these animals.

Goodall has written more than 20 books about chimpanzees. She has made 18 films about her work with them. She started the Jane Goodall Institute in Connecticut to help with wildlife research, education, and conservation. She started a program for children, too. It is called Roots & Shoots. Its goal is to help young people make a difference for people, animals, and the environment.

Goodall has been given many awards and honors for her work. She travels around the world to talk to people about protecting the environment.

Source 3: Elizabeth Blackwell – First Woman U.S. Doctor
by Carmen Santos

"It is not easy to be a pioneer — but oh, it is exciting! I would not trade one moment, even the worst moment, for all the riches in the world." –Elizabeth Blackwell

What did Elizabeth Blackwell mean when she said these words? Why did she think she was a pioneer? What could be so exciting?

Early Years of Her Life

Elizabeth Blackwell was born in England on February 3, 1821. She had four brothers and four sisters. When Elizabeth was eleven years old, her father decided to move the family to America. The voyage took seven weeks. The family lived in New York and New Jersey.

Idea of Becoming a Doctor

One of Elizabeth's friends was very sick. She told Elizabeth that she really wished there were women doctors. She thought women doctors would be kind and caring. That was when Elizabeth decided that she should be a doctor to help women like her friend.

However, medical school cost a lot. It would be about $3,000. She saved up all of her money from teaching.

Studying Medicine

Elizabeth tried to get into a college to study. Many colleges did not accept her because she was a woman. A woman had not studied medicine before.

She had to apply to 30 colleges until a college in New York finally accepted her. She began her new life as a student at the age of 26.

First Work as a Doctor

Elizabeth worked in London, England, and France and got lots of experience. Later, she returned to New York City. When no hospital would hire a woman, she opened up her own doctor's office.

One of her sisters became a doctor, too. Together they worked at a clinic for needy women and children. When they got enough money, they built a hospital. People began to respect Elizabeth. They saw the good work her hospital did. The hospital also helped train many nurses.

Elizabeth then opened up a medical school for women in New York. Fifteen students were in the first class. There were nine teachers. The school would expand and teach more students each year.

Later Years of Her Life

Elizabeth returned to England and set up another clinic. Her sister stayed in New York to run the medical school. Elizabeth was an instructor at the London School of Medicine for Women. She really loved teaching others about medicine. She liked helping women follow their dreams of becoming doctors.

Elizabeth wrote several books. One book described her work as a doctor. It was titled *Pioneer Work in Opening the Medical Field to Women*. She wrote about herself in this autobiography.

Elizabeth Blackwell, a True Pioneer

Elizabeth Blackwell was indeed a pioneer, someone who opens up and explores a new area. For Elizabeth, that area was medicine. She studied medicine when many people felt women should not. Because of her work, more and more women became doctors.

Writing Prompt

Write an informative essay about how many people who have achieved great things have followed their passions. Use information from the passages in your essay.

Be sure to include

- an introduction;
- information from the passages as support; and
- a conclusion that is related to the information presented.

_____

_____

_____

_____

_____

_____

_____

_____

_____

_____

_____

_____

_____

_____

_____

END OF PRACTICE SET

ANSWER KEY

Indiana Academic Standards

The Indiana Academic Standards describe what students are expected to know. Student learning throughout the year is based on these standards, and all the questions on the ILEARN assessments cover these standards. All the exercises and questions in this book cover the Indiana Academic Standards.

Standards Assessed

The standards assessed on the test are divided into the following areas:

- Reading Standards: Literature
- Reading Standards: Nonfiction
- Reading Standards: Vocabulary
- Writing Standards: Writing Genres (Persuasive, Informative, and Narrative)
- Writing Standards: Writing Process
- Writing Standards: Research Process
- Writing Standards: Conventions of Standard English

Within each of these areas, there are standards that describe specific skills the student should have. The answer key that follows lists the standard assessed by each question.

Scoring Short Answer Questions and Writing Tasks

This practice book includes short answer questions, where students provide a written answer to a question. The answer key gives guidance on how to score these questions and lists what should be included in the answer.

The writing tasks in this workbook are scored based on rubrics that list the features expected of student writing. These features are based on the state standards and are the same criteria used when scoring writing tasks on assessments. The rubric used for scoring these questions is included in the back of this book. Use the rubric to score these questions, and as a guide for giving the student advice on how to improve an answer.

Practice Set 1

Question	Answer	Indiana Academic Standard
1	A	Apply context clues (e.g., word, phrase, and sentence clues) and text features (e.g., maps, illustrations, charts) to determine the meanings of unknown words.
2	C	Identify relationships among words, including synonyms, antonyms, homographs, homonyms, and multiple-meaning words (e.g., puzzle, fire).
3	See Below	Ask and answer questions to demonstrate understanding of a text, referring explicitly to the text as the basis for the answers.
4	D	Retell folktales, fables, and tall tales from diverse cultures; identify the themes in these works.
5	A	Ask and answer questions to demonstrate understanding of a text, referring explicitly to the text as the basis for the answers.
6	C	Determine how the author uses words and phrases to provide meaning to works of literature, distinguishing literal from nonliteral language, including figurative language.
7	D	Read and comprehend a variety of literature.
8	B	Describe characters in a story (e.g., their traits, motivations, or feelings) and explain how their actions contribute to the plot.
9	A	Describe characters in a story (e.g., their traits, motivations, or feelings) and explain how their actions contribute to the plot.
10	C	Retell folktales, fables, and tall tales from diverse cultures; identify the themes in these works.
11	See Below	Retell folktales, fables, and tall tales from diverse cultures; identify the themes in these works.
12	See Below	Distinguish personal point of view from that of the narrator or those of the characters.

Q3.
Give a score of 0, 1, or 2 based on how well the answer meets the criteria listed below.
- The web should be completed with three examples from the passage of things that Sarah and Janet compete over.
- Answers include singing, running fast, playing volleyball, reading fast, and choosing clothes.

Q11.
Give a score of 0, 1, or 2 based on how well the answer meets the criteria listed below.
- It should give a reasonable explanation of why the student chose the title.
- It should relate the title to the theme of the passage.
- It should use relevant details from the passage.

Q12.
Give a score of 0, 1, or 2 based on how well the answer meets the criteria listed below.
- It should give a reasonable description of how the girls competing could be good for them.
- The answer may refer to how it makes the girls try harder or how it encourages them to do better.

Practice Set 2

Question	Answer	Indiana Academic Standard
1	C	Determine how the author uses words and phrases to provide meaning to works of literature, distinguishing literal from nonliteral language, including figurative language.
2	B	Describe characters in a story (e.g., their traits, motivations, or feelings) and explain how their actions contribute to the plot.
3	D	Describe characters in a story (e.g., their traits, motivations, or feelings) and explain how their actions contribute to the plot.
4	See Below	Ask and answer questions to demonstrate understanding of a text, referring explicitly to the text as the basis for the answers.
5	A	Determine how the author uses words and phrases to provide meaning to works of literature, distinguishing literal from nonliteral language, including figurative language.
6	D	Distinguish personal point of view from that of the narrator or those of the characters.
7	B	Retell folktales, fables, and tall tales from diverse cultures; identify the themes in these works.
8	C	Apply context clues (e.g., word, phrase, and sentence clues) and text features (e.g., maps, illustrations, charts) to determine the meanings of unknown words.
9	afraid brave	Describe characters in a story (e.g., their traits, motivations, or feelings) and explain how their actions contribute to the plot.
10	See Below	Distinguish personal point of view from that of the narrator or those of the characters.
11	See Below	Describe characters in a story (e.g., their traits, motivations, or feelings) and explain how their actions contribute to the plot.

Q4.
Give a score of 0, 1, or 2 based on how many relevant details are listed. Possible answers are listed below.
- He is quiet as they drive into the city. / He gasps when he looks up at the tower. / His stomach turns over. / He says that he's not sure if he can do it. / He takes a deep breath as he steps through the entrance. / He holds his father's hand.

Q10.
Give a score of 0, 1, or 2 based on how well the answer meets the criteria listed below.
- It should make a reasonable inference about how Toby feels at the end of the passage.
- The inference could be that he feels proud of himself, unafraid, or relieved.
- It should use relevant details from the passage.

Q11.
Give a score of 0, 1, or 2 based on how well the answer meets the criteria listed below.
- It should identify Toby's problem as that he has a fear of heights.
- It should describe how Toby faces his fear by climbing to the top of the Eiffel Tower.
- It should use relevant details from the passage.

Practice Set 3

Question	Answer	Indiana Academic Standard
1	D	Use a known word as a clue to the meaning of an unknown word with the same root, and identify when an affix is added to a known root word.
2	C	Describe the relationship between a series of historical events, scientific ideas or concepts, or steps in processes or procedures in a text, using words such as first, next, finally, because, problem, solution, same, and different.
3	B	Determine the main idea of a text; recount the key details and explain how they support the main idea.
4	A	Identify relationships among words, including synonyms, antonyms, homographs, homonyms, and multiple-meaning words (e.g., puzzle, fire).
5	C	Apply knowledge of text features to locate information and gain meaning from a text (e.g., maps, illustrations, charts, font/format).
6	B	Describe the relationship between a series of historical events, scientific ideas or concepts, or steps in processes or procedures in a text, using words such as first, next, finally, because, problem, solution, same, and different.
7	B	Apply knowledge of text features to locate information and gain meaning from a text (e.g., maps, illustrations, charts, font/format).
8	"suggest a lower price"	Apply context clues (e.g., word, phrase, and sentence clues) and text features (e.g., maps, illustrations, charts) to determine the meanings of unknown words.
9	See Below	Apply knowledge of text features to locate information and gain meaning from a text (e.g., maps, illustrations, charts, font/format).
10	See Below	Identify how a nonfiction text can be structured to indicate a problem and solution or to put events in chronological order.
11	See Below	Distinguish one's own perspective from that of the author of the text.
12	See Below	Describe the relationship between a series of historical events, scientific ideas or concepts, or steps in processes or procedures in a text, using words such as first, next, finally, because, problem, solution, same, and different.
13	See Below	Write persuasive compositions in a variety of forms.

Q9.
Give a score of 0, 1, or 2 based on how many relevant examples are given.
- The answer could refer to the items shown, the way the items are displayed, or the poster.

Q10.
Give a score of 0.5 for each sentence correctly matched with its purpose. The correct matches are listed below.
- A yard sale is when you sell items in your front yard. → to tell what a yard sale is
- People have yard sales to get rid of unwanted items. → to give the main reason for having a yard sale
- It can also be a good way to make some extra money. → to give a second reason for having a yard sale
- Here are some tips on how to have a good yard sale. → to tell what the passage is about

Q11.
Give a score of 0, 1, or 2 based on how well the answer meets the criteria listed below.
- It should give a reasonable explanation of why asking other people to join in would be a good idea.
- The benefits may include having more items to sell, having help to run it, or making more money.

Q12.
Give a score of 1 for each column completed correctly. The correct matches are listed below.
- The Week Before Your Yard Sale → put up flyers, tell your friends, run a newspaper ad
- On the Day of Your Yard Sale → put balloons up, set up the tables, put a sign in your street

Q13. Use the Opinion Writing Rubric at the end of the answer key to give an overall score out of 10.

Practice Set 4

Question	Answer	Indiana Academic Standard
1	C	Apply context clues (e.g., word, phrase, and sentence clues) and text features (e.g., maps, illustrations, charts) to determine the meanings of unknown words.
2	A	Apply knowledge of text features to locate information and gain meaning from a text (e.g., maps, illustrations, charts, font/format).
3	A	Distinguish among the purposes of various media messages, including for information, entertainment, persuasion, interpretation of events, or transmission of culture.
4	Step 1	Describe the relationship between a series of historical events, scientific ideas or concepts, or steps in processes or procedures in a text, using words such as first, next, finally, because, problem, solution, same, and different.
5	B	Identify relationships among words, including synonyms, antonyms, homographs, homonyms, and multiple-meaning words (e.g., puzzle, fire).
6	See Below	Describe the relationship between a series of historical events, scientific ideas or concepts, or steps in processes or procedures in a text, using words such as first, next, finally, because, problem, solution, same, and different.
7	C	Ask and answer questions to demonstrate understanding of a text, referring explicitly to the text as the basis for the answers.
8	B	Distinguish among the purposes of various media messages, including for information, entertainment, persuasion, interpretation of events, or transmission of culture.
9	See Below	Determine the main idea of a text; recount the key details and explain how they support the main idea.
10	See Below	Describe the relationship between a series of historical events, scientific ideas or concepts, or steps in processes or procedures in a text, using words such as first, next, finally, because, problem, solution, same, and different.
11	See Below	Distinguish one's own perspective from that of the author of the text.
12	See Below	Write informative compositions on a variety of topics.

Q6.
Give a score of 0, 1, or 2 based on how well the answer meets the criteria listed below.
- The diagram should be completed with each sentence in the correct place, as below.
- It is too sour. → Add sugar. / It is too sweet. → Add lemon juice. / It is too strong. → Add water.

Q9.
Give a score of 0, 1, or 2 based on how many relevant examples are given.
- Any reasonable answer can be accepted as long as it is based on information in the passage.
- The student may refer to setting up a lemonade at the friend's house, having help to make the lemonade, having someone to help decorate the stand, or selling other products the friend makes.

Q10.
The student should complete the chart in the order below. Give a score of 0.5 for each item correctly ordered.
- sugar → boiling water → lemon juice → cold water

Q11.
Give a score of 0, 1, or 2 based on how well the answer meets the criteria listed below.
- It should state whether or not the student feels it would be worth it to make lemonade.
- It should provide a fully-supported explanation of why or why not.

Q12. Use the Informative Writing Rubric at the end of the answer key to give an overall score out of 10.

Practice Set 5

Question	Answer	Indiana Academic Standard
1	B	Recognize the meanings of idioms in context.
2	C	Ask and answer questions to demonstrate understanding of a text, referring explicitly to the text as the basis for the answers.
3	B	Use terms such as chapter, scene, and stanza to refer to the parts of stories, plays, and poems; describe how each successive part builds on earlier sections.
4	A	Distinguish personal point of view from that of the narrator or those of the characters.
5	B	Ask and answer questions to demonstrate understanding of a text, referring explicitly to the text as the basis for the answers.
6	See Below	Ask and answer questions to demonstrate understanding of a text, referring explicitly to the text as the basis for the answers.
7	D	Ask and answer questions to demonstrate understanding of a text, referring explicitly to the text as the basis for the answers.
8	B	Determine how the author uses words and phrases to provide meaning to works of literature, distinguishing literal from nonliteral language, including figurative language.
9	B	Ask and answer questions to demonstrate understanding of a text, referring explicitly to the text as the basis for the answers.
10	C	Explain how specific aspects of a text's illustrations contribute to what is conveyed by the words in a story.
11	See Below	Describe characters in a story (e.g., their traits, motivations, or feelings) and explain how their actions contribute to the plot.
12	See Below	Write narrative compositions in a variety of forms.

Q6.
Give a score of 0, 1, or 2 based on how many relevant details are given.
- Possible details could refer to how she paces up and down, how she keeps asking where he is, how she searches the crowd, or how she stands tall to try to see every person coming through the gate.

Q11.
Give a score of 0, 1, or 2 based on how well the answer meets the criteria listed below.
- It should provide a reasonable analysis of what the father's actions show about how he feels.
- It may refer to how he drops his bags or to how he sweeps his daughters into his arms.
- It should describe how he feels excited, overjoyed, or relieved.

Q12. Use the Narrative Writing Rubric at the end of the answer key to give an overall score out of 10.

Practice Set 6

Question	Answer	Indiana Academic Standard
1	B	Identify relationships among words, including synonyms, antonyms, homographs, homonyms, and multiple-meaning words (e.g., puzzle, fire).
2	amazing beautiful	Distinguish personal point of view from that of the narrator or those of the characters.
3	A	Use terms such as chapter, scene, and stanza to refer to the parts of stories, plays, and poems; describe how each successive part builds on earlier sections.
4	C	Determine how the author uses words and phrases to provide meaning to works of literature, distinguishing literal from nonliteral language, including figurative language.
5	B	Ask and answer questions to demonstrate understanding of a text, referring explicitly to the text as the basis for the answers.
6	See Below	Determine how the author uses words and phrases to provide meaning to works of literature, distinguishing literal from nonliteral language, including figurative language.
7	See Below	Ask and answer questions to demonstrate understanding of a text, referring explicitly to the text as the basis for the answers.
8	See Below	Distinguish personal point of view from that of the narrator or those of the characters.
9	See Below	Ask and answer questions to demonstrate understanding of a text, referring explicitly to the text as the basis for the answers.
10	C	Distinguish personal point of view from that of the narrator or those of the characters.

Q6.
Give a score of 0, 1, or 2 based on how lines are correctly selected. The correct lines are listed below.
- "with slow and steady ease" and "in the earth all wet and warm."

Q7.
Give a score of 0, 1, or 2 based on how well the answer meets the criteria listed below.
- It should give a reasonable explanation of how a worm is like an explorer.
- It should include a description of how worms explore under the ground.
- It should use relevant details from the poem.

Q8.
Give a score of 0, 1, or 2 based on how well the answer meets the criteria listed below.
- It should give an opinion on whether the poet is successful at showing readers that worms are interesting and special.
- It should provide a fully-supported explanation to support the opinion.

Q9.
Give a score of 0, 1, or 2 based on how well the answer meets the criteria listed below.
- It should show an understanding that the worm has a simple form or a "single beautiful shape."
- It should use relevant details from the poem.

Practice Set 7

Question	Answer	Indiana Academic Standard
1	C	Ask and answer questions to demonstrate understanding of a text, referring explicitly to the text as the basis for the answers.
2	A	Determine how the author uses words and phrases to provide meaning to works of literature, distinguishing literal from nonliteral language, including figurative language.
3	C	Use terms such as chapter, scene, and stanza to refer to the parts of stories, plays, and poems; describe how each successive part builds on earlier sections.
4	C	Determine how the author uses words and phrases to provide meaning to works of literature, distinguishing literal from nonliteral language, including figurative language.
5	D	Apply context clues (e.g., word, phrase, and sentence clues) and text features (e.g., maps, illustrations, charts) to determine the meanings of unknown words.
6	D	Ask and answer questions to demonstrate understanding of a text, referring explicitly to the text as the basis for the answers.
7	See Below	Explain how specific aspects of a text's illustrations contribute to what is conveyed by the words in a story.
8	See Below	Ask and answer questions to demonstrate understanding of a text, referring explicitly to the text as the basis for the answers.
9	See Below	Ask and answer questions to demonstrate understanding of a text, referring explicitly to the text as the basis for the answers.
10	See Below	Distinguish personal point of view from that of the narrator or those of the characters.

Q7.
Give a score of 0, 1, or 2 based on how well the answer meets the criteria listed below.
- It should provide a reasonable description of what the photograph helps readers understand.
- The answer could refer to how the photograph shows how bees make honey or to how it shows how beekeepers protect themselves.

Q8.
Give a score of 0, 1, or 2 based on how well the answer meets the criteria listed below.
- The web should be completed with three facts from the passage about bees.
- Any detail included in the poem or caption can be accepted as long as it is factual and not an opinion.

Q9.
Give a score of 0, 1, or 2 based on how well the answer meets the criteria listed below.
- It should provide a reasonable explanation of whether or not people need to fear bees. Either answer is acceptable as long as it is supported.
- The answer may refer to how bees do not wish to harm, how bees usually only sting when they are afraid, or how leaving bees alone keeps you safe from them.
- The answer may refer to how many bees can be dangerous or how beekeepers need to wear safety suits.

Q10.
Give a score of 0, 1, or 2 based on how well the answer meets the criteria listed below.
- It should provide a reasonable analysis of how the point of view affects the poem.
- The answer should include an explanation of how the point of view influences whether or not readers can take the poem seriously.

Practice Set 8

Question	Answer	Indiana Academic Standard
1	A	Recognize the meanings of idioms in context.
2	A	Identify relationships among words, including synonyms, antonyms, homographs, homonyms, and multiple-meaning words (e.g., puzzle, fire).
3	D	Ask and answer questions to demonstrate understanding of a text, referring explicitly to the text as the basis for the answers.
4	See Below	Ask and answer questions to demonstrate understanding of a text, referring explicitly to the text as the basis for the answers.
5	See Below	Apply knowledge of text features to locate information and gain meaning from a text (e.g., maps, illustrations, charts, font/format).
6	C	Distinguish one's own perspective from that of the author of the text.
7	A	Determine the main idea of a text; recount the key details and explain how they support the main idea.
8	C	Apply knowledge of text features to locate information and gain meaning from a text (e.g., maps, illustrations, charts, font/format).
9	See Below	Distinguish between fact and opinion; explain how an author uses reasons and facts to support specific points in a text.
10	See Below	Distinguish one's own perspective from that of the author of the text.
11	See Below	Write informative compositions on a variety of topics.

Q4.
Give a score of 0, 1, or 2 based on how well the answer meets the criteria listed below.
- Any of the last 4 sentences can be accepted.
- The student should provide a reasonable explanation of why the two sentences were chosen and how they show the reason for writing the letter.

Q5.
Give a score of 1 for each book added to the table correctly. The correct books are listed below.
- Favorite Book: *The Shining Light*
- First Book Read: *The Singing Swordfish*

Q9.
Give a score of 0, 1, or 2 based on how many relevant reasons are given.
- Possible reasons include that it was well-written, that the pictures were good, or that it made him laugh.

Q10.
Give a score of 0, 1, or 2 based on how well the answer meets the criteria listed below.
- It should give an opinion on whether or not Simeon would feel good after reading the letter.
- It should provide a fully-supported explanation to support the opinion.

Q11. Use the Informative Writing Rubric at the end of the answer key to give an overall score out of 10.

Practice Set 9

Question	Answer	Indiana Academic Standard
1	C	Use a known word as a clue to the meaning of an unknown word with the same root, and identify when an affix is added to a known root word.
2	B	Apply context clues (e.g., word, phrase, and sentence clues) and text features (e.g., maps, illustrations, charts) to determine the meanings of unknown words.
3	C	Ask and answer questions to demonstrate understanding of a text, referring explicitly to the text as the basis for the answers.
4	A	Determine the main idea of a text; recount the key details and explain how they support the main idea.
5	D	Determine the main idea of a text; recount the key details and explain how they support the main idea.
6	A	Identify how a nonfiction text can be structured to indicate a problem and solution or to put events in chronological order.
7	Standing up for yourself	Apply knowledge of text features to locate information and gain meaning from a text (e.g., maps, illustrations, charts, font/format).
8	C	Distinguish one's own perspective from that of the author of the text.
9	See Below	Distinguish between fact and opinion; explain how an author uses reasons and facts to support specific points in a text.
10	See Below	Write persuasive compositions in a variety of forms.

Q9.
Give a score of 0, 1, or 2 based on how well the answer meets the criteria listed below.
- It should describe the benefits of increasing the length of the lunch break.
- The benefits described should be based on the argument from the passage.
- It should use relevant details from the passage.

Q10.
Give a score of 0, 1, or 2 based on how well the answer meets the criteria listed below.
- Each paragraph should use the benefit listed to persuade the principle to increase the length of the lunch break.
- Each paragraph should be persuasive and should explain why the benefit listed would help students or teachers.

Practice Set 10

Question	Answer	Indiana Academic Standard
1	C	Apply context clues (e.g., word, phrase, and sentence clues) and text features (e.g., maps, illustrations, charts) to determine the meanings of unknown words.
2	famous well-known	Identify relationships among words, including synonyms, antonyms, homographs, homonyms, and multiple-meaning words (e.g., puzzle, fire).
3	A	Describe characters in a story (e.g., their traits, motivations, or feelings) and explain how their actions contribute to the plot.
4	B	Determine how the author uses words and phrases to provide meaning to works of literature, distinguishing literal from nonliteral language, including figurative language.
5	From top to bottom: 3, 2, 4, 1	Use terms such as chapter, scene, and stanza to refer to the parts of stories, plays, and poems; describe how each successive part builds on earlier sections.
6	B	Distinguish personal point of view from that of the narrator or those of the characters.
7	C	Use terms such as chapter, scene, and stanza to refer to the parts of stories, plays, and poems; describe how each successive part builds on earlier sections.
8	D	Describe characters in a story (e.g., their traits, motivations, or feelings) and explain how their actions contribute to the plot.
9	Sentences 3 and 4	Ask and answer questions to demonstrate understanding of a text, referring explicitly to the text as the basis for the answers.
10	See Below	Retell folktales, fables, and tall tales from diverse cultures; identify the themes in these works.
11	See Below	Describe characters in a story (e.g., their traits, motivations, or feelings) and explain how their actions contribute to the plot.
12	See Below	Write narrative compositions in a variety of forms.

Q10.
Give a score of 0, 1, or 2 based on how well the answer meets the criteria listed below.
- It should describe the lesson that Kevin learns in the story. The lesson should be not to be mean to others, to focus on being known for something positive, or how being funny can become nasty.
- It should use relevant details from the passage.

Q11.
Give a score of 0, 1, or 2 based on how well the answer meets the criteria listed below.
- It should make a prediction about whether or not Kevin will keep playing jokes.
- It should provide a fully-supported explanation to support the prediction.
- It should use relevant details from the passage.

Q12. Use the Narrative Writing Rubric at the end of the answer key to give an overall score out of 10.

Practice Set 11

Question	Answer	Indiana Academic Standard
1	See Below	Conduct short research on a topic. Locate information in reference texts, electronic resources, or through interviews.
2	See Below	Conduct short research on a topic. Locate information in reference texts, electronic resources, or through interviews.
3	See Below	Write persuasive compositions in a variety of forms that state the opinion in an introductory statement or section.
4	See Below	Write persuasive compositions in a variety of forms that support the opinion with reasons in an organized way.
5	B	Edit writing for format and convention. Demonstrate command of English grammar and usage.
6	C	Edit writing for format and convention. Demonstrate command of capitalization, punctuation, and spelling.
7	D	Edit writing for format and convention. Demonstrate command of English grammar and usage.
8	A	Edit writing for format and convention. Demonstrate command of English grammar and usage.
9	tomorrow	Edit writing for format and convention. Demonstrate command of capitalization, punctuation, and spelling.
10	A	Edit writing for format and convention. Demonstrate command of English grammar and usage.
11	B	Edit writing for format and convention. Demonstrate command of capitalization, punctuation, and spelling.
12	B	Edit writing for format and convention. Demonstrate command of English grammar and usage.
13	A	Edit writing for format and convention. Demonstrate command of capitalization, punctuation, and spelling.
14	South America	Edit writing for format and convention. Demonstrate command of capitalization, punctuation, and spelling.
15	interesting	Edit writing for format and convention. Demonstrate command of capitalization, punctuation, and spelling.
16	D	Edit writing for format and convention. Demonstrate command of capitalization, punctuation, and spelling.
17	D	Edit writing for format and convention. Demonstrate command of English grammar and usage.
18	C	Edit writing for format and convention. Demonstrate command of capitalization, punctuation, and spelling.
19	A	Edit writing for format and convention. Demonstrate command of English grammar and usage.
20	A	Edit writing for format and convention. Demonstrate command of capitalization, punctuation, and spelling.
21	"I guess it's not that simple," said the donkey.	Edit writing for format and convention. Demonstrate command of capitalization, punctuation, and spelling.
22	C	Revise to improve writing.

Q1.
Give a score of 1 for circling a correct sentence. Either of the following two sentences may be circled.
- They are named for their habit of landing on people and licking the sweat from the skin.
- The bees do this to take in the salt in the sweat.

Q2.
Give a score of 0, 1, or 2 based on how well the answer meets the criteria listed below.
- It should list five details mentioned in the passage that could be used to identify sweat bees.
- Any of the details below could be listed.
- They lick sweat from people's skin. / They are small to medium in size. / They are from 4 to 10 mm long. / They are black or brownish. / Some are bright metallic green. / Some have brassy yellow or red markings. / Males can have yellow faces.

Q3.
Give a score of 0, 1, or 2 based on how well the answer meets the criteria listed below.
- The student should write a reasonable opening that introduces the topic and states the main idea.
- The sentence should show an understanding that the main idea is about the area outside the school being dangerous for students.

Q4.
Give a score of 0, 1, or 2 based on how well the answer meets the criteria listed below.
- Two details should be listed that support the idea that the situation is dangerous.
- The details listed should be relevant to the topic of students being in danger because of the roads near the school or because of cars driving too fast near the school.

Practice Set 12

Question	Answer	Indiana Academic Standard
1	C	Apply context clues (e.g., word, phrase, and sentence clues) and text features (e.g., maps, illustrations, charts) to determine the meanings of unknown words.
2	A	Determine the meanings of general academic and content-specific words and phrases in a nonfiction text.
3	B	Ask and answer questions to demonstrate understanding of a text, referring explicitly to the text as the basis for the answers.
4	A	Identify how a nonfiction text can be structured to indicate a problem and solution or to put events in chronological order.
5	B	Determine the main idea of a text; recount the key details and explain how they support the main idea.
6	See Below	Determine the main idea of a text; recount the key details and explain how they support the main idea.
7	See Below	Distinguish between fact and opinion; explain how an author uses reasons and facts to support specific points in a text.
8	B	Describe the relationship between a series of historical events, scientific ideas or concepts, or steps in processes or procedures in a text, using words such as first, next, finally, because, problem, solution, same, and different.
9	B	Distinguish one's own perspective from that of the author of the text.
10	D	Identify relationships among words, including synonyms, antonyms, homographs, homonyms, and multiple-meaning words (e.g., puzzle, fire).
11	See Below	Describe the relationship between a series of historical events, scientific ideas or concepts, or steps in processes or procedures in a text, using words such as first, next, finally, because, problem, solution, same, and different.
12	See Below	Distinguish between fact and opinion; explain how an author uses reasons and facts to support specific points in a text.

Q6.
Give a score of 0, 1, or 2 based on how many relevant supporting details are given.

- The supporting details listed could be that Rafael Nadal beat Roger Federer at Wimbledon in 2008 and 2010, that Nadal beat Roger in 6 out of 8 Grand Slam finals, that Nadal became world number one, or that Roger will have to beat Nadal to become number one again.

Q7.
Give a score of 0, 1, or 2 based on how well the answer meets the criteria listed below.

- The second and third sentences should be circled.
- Any factual detail from the passage can be accepted.

Q11.
Give a score of 0, 1, or 2 based on how well the answer meets the criteria listed below.

- It should provide a reasonable explanation of why the 2008 Wimbledon final was important.
- It should include two reasons that the final was important. Possible reasons could refer to how Nadal stopped Roger from winning six times, how it was a tough match, how it started a row between them, or how some people think it was the best match ever played.

Q12.
Give a score of 0, 1, or 2 based on how well the answer meets the criteria listed below.

- It should use relevant details to explain how the author shows that Federer is a successful tennis player.
- The details may include that he has been the world number one, that he was world number one for 237 weeks, that he has won 16 Grand Slam finals, or that he has won Wimbledon six times.

Practice Set 13

Question	Answer	Indiana Academic Standard
1	B	Identify relationships among words, including synonyms, antonyms, homographs, homonyms, and multiple-meaning words (e.g., puzzle, fire).
2	decision choice	Identify relationships among words, including synonyms, antonyms, homographs, homonyms, and multiple-meaning words (e.g., puzzle, fire).
3	third pair	Ask and answer questions to demonstrate understanding of a text, referring explicitly to the text as the basis for the answers.
4	A	Describe characters in a story (e.g., their traits, motivations, or feelings) and explain how their actions contribute to the plot.
5	A	Determine how the author uses words and phrases to provide meaning to works of literature, distinguishing literal from nonliteral language, including figurative language.
6	A	Describe characters in a story (e.g., their traits, motivations, or feelings) and explain how their actions contribute to the plot.
7	A	Use terms such as chapter, scene, and stanza to refer to the parts of stories, plays, and poems; describe how each successive part builds on earlier sections.
8	See Below	Ask and answer questions to demonstrate understanding of a text, referring explicitly to the text as the basis for the answers.
9	D	Distinguish personal point of view from that of the narrator or those of the characters.
10	See Below	Describe characters in a story (e.g., their traits, motivations, or feelings) and explain how their actions contribute to the plot.
11	See Below	Use terms such as chapter, scene, and stanza to refer to the parts of stories, plays, and poems; describe how each successive part builds on earlier sections.
12	See Below	Distinguish personal point of view from that of the narrator or those of the characters.

Q8.
Give a score of 0, 1, or 2 based on how well the answer meets the criteria listed below.
- It should provide a reasonable explanation of why the last paragraph is important to the main idea.
- The answer should refer to how the last paragraph shows that Steven's bold decision paid off.

Q10.
Give a score of 0, 1, or 2 based on how well the answer meets the criteria listed below.
- It should make a reasonable prediction about whether Steven team's would have won without him.
- Any prediction can be accepted as long as it is explained and supported with details from the passage.

Q11.
Give a score of 0, 1, or 2 based on how well the answer meets the criteria listed below.
- It should provide an analysis of what the paragraph reveals about Steven.
- The answer may refer to how it shows that he knew playing was a risk to himself, how he thought carefully about his decision, or how he put the needs of his team first.

Q12.
Give a score of 0, 1, or 2 based on how well the answer meets the criteria listed below.
- It should give an opinion about whether or not Steven did the right thing.
- The opinion should include a reasonable explanation to support it.

Practice Set 14

Question	Answer	Indiana Academic Standard
1	B	Determine the meanings of general academic and content-specific words and phrases in a nonfiction text.
2	B	Apply knowledge of text features to locate information and gain meaning from a text (e.g., maps, illustrations, charts, font/format).
3	A	Describe the relationship between a series of historical events, scientific ideas or concepts, or steps in processes or procedures in a text, using words such as first, next, finally, because, problem, solution, same, and different.
4	A	Determine the main idea of a text; recount the key details and explain how they support the main idea.
5	B	Determine the meanings of general academic and content-specific words and phrases in a nonfiction text.
6	Step 3	Describe the relationship between a series of historical events, scientific ideas or concepts, or steps in processes or procedures in a text, using words such as first, next, finally, because, problem, solution, same, and different.
7	C	Apply knowledge of text features to locate information and gain meaning from a text (e.g., maps, illustrations, charts, font/format).
8	B	Apply knowledge of text features to locate information and gain meaning from a text (e.g., maps, illustrations, charts, font/format).
9	A	Read and comprehend a variety of nonfiction.
10	See Below	Apply knowledge of text features to locate information and gain meaning from a text (e.g., maps, illustrations, charts, font/format).
11	See Below	Distinguish between fact and opinion; explain how an author uses reasons and facts to support specific points in a text.
12	See Below	Ask and answer questions to demonstrate understanding of a text, referring explicitly to the text as the basis for the answers.
13	See Below	Write persuasive compositions in a variety of forms.

Q10.
Give a score of 0, 1, or 2 based on how many acceptable features are listed.
- Any feature that helps show that the passage is a recipe can be accepted.
- The features could be broad, such as that the passage tells how to make a food or gives directions.
- The features could be specific, such as that the passage has a section titled "What to Do," has steps to follow, or includes a picture of making food.

Q11.
Give a score of 0, 1, or 2 based on how many correct reasons are given.
- Possible answers include that children like them, that they are crunchy, that the flavor is a hit, or that they are easy to make.

Q12.
Give a score of 0, 1, or 2 based on how well the answer meets the criteria listed below.
- It should identify three tasks that would have to be done carefully and give a reasonable explanation of why you have to be careful and what you have to do to stop things going wrong.
- The three tasks could be based on softening the butter in step 2, cleaning your hands before mixing in step 2, not getting water in the chocolate in step 4, letting the chocolate cool in step 5, or making sure the rice crispy cake is covered in chocolate in step 5.

Q13. Use the Opinion Writing Rubric at the end of the answer key to give an overall score out of 10.

Practice Set 15

Question	Answer	Indiana Academic Standard
1	C	Apply context clues (e.g., word, phrase, and sentence clues) and text features (e.g., maps, illustrations, charts) to determine the meanings of unknown words.
2	C	Identify relationships among words, including synonyms, antonyms, homographs, homonyms, and multiple-meaning words (e.g., puzzle, fire).
3	A	Ask and answer questions to demonstrate understanding of a text, referring explicitly to the text as the basis for the answers.
4	B	Describe the relationship between a series of historical events, scientific ideas or concepts, or steps in processes or procedures in a text, using words such as first, next, finally, because, problem, solution, same, and different.
5	B	Read and comprehend a variety of nonfiction.
6	D	Determine the main idea of a text; recount the key details and explain how they support the main idea.
7	See Below	Ask and answer questions to demonstrate understanding of a text, referring explicitly to the text as the basis for the answers.
8	A	Identify relationships among words, including synonyms, antonyms, homographs, homonyms, and multiple-meaning words (e.g., puzzle, fire).
9	See Below	Distinguish between fact and opinion; explain how an author uses reasons and facts to support specific points in a text.
10	See Below	Describe the relationship between a series of historical events, scientific ideas or concepts, or steps in processes or procedures in a text, using words such as first, next, finally, because, problem, solution, same, and different.
11	See Below	Distinguish one's own perspective from that of the author of the text.
12	See Below	Write informative compositions on a variety of topics.

Q7.
Give a score of 0.5 for each section correctly listed. The possible sections are listed below.
- news, sport, home, travel, food, art, fashion, movies, or puzzles

Q9.
Give a score of 0, 1, or 2 based on how well the answer meets the criteria listed below.
- It should provide a reasonable explanation of the importance of the second sentence.
- The answer should show an understanding that the detail explains what a Pulitzer Prize is, shows the meaning of winning a Pulitzer Prize, or shows that *The New York Times* is known for excellent reporting.

Q10.
Give a score of 0, 1, or 2 based on how many correct differences are given.
- Possible answers include that it now costs more, that it sells fewer copies than it once did, or that it has to compete with online sites that offer news for free.

Q11.
Give a score of 0, 1, or 2 based on how well the answer meets the criteria listed below.
- It should state which details the student found most interesting.
- It should provide a fully-supported explanation of why the student found those details interesting.

Q12. Use the Informative Writing Rubric at the end of the answer key to give an overall score out of 10.

Practice Set 16

Question	Answer	Indiana Academic Standard
1	B	Apply context clues (e.g., word, phrase, and sentence clues) and text features (e.g., maps, illustrations, charts) to determine the meanings of unknown words.
2	C	Determine how the author uses words and phrases to provide meaning to works of literature, distinguishing literal from nonliteral language, including figurative language.
3	2	Use terms such as chapter, scene, and stanza to refer to the parts of stories, plays, and poems; describe how each successive part builds on earlier sections.
4	A	Determine how the author uses words and phrases to provide meaning to works of literature, distinguishing literal from nonliteral language, including figurative language.
5	C	Use terms such as chapter, scene, and stanza to refer to the parts of stories, plays, and poems; describe how each successive part builds on earlier sections.
6	C	Use terms such as chapter, scene, and stanza to refer to the parts of stories, plays, and poems; describe how each successive part builds on earlier sections.
7	A	Read and comprehend a variety of literature.
8	little mighty	Determine how the author uses words and phrases to provide meaning to works of literature, distinguishing literal from nonliteral language, including figurative language.
9	See Below	Read and comprehend a variety of literature.
10	See Below	Explain how specific aspects of a text's illustrations contribute to what is conveyed by the words in a story.
11	See Below	Ask and answer questions to demonstrate understanding of a text, referring explicitly to the text as the basis for the answers.
12	See Below	Write narrative compositions in a variety of forms.

Q9.
Give a score of 0, 1, or 2 based on how well the answer meets the criteria listed below.

- It should explain that water, sand, and minutes all make up something much larger than themselves.

Q10.
Give a score of 0, 1, or 2 based on how well the answer meets the criteria listed below.

- It should identify the main idea as being about how little things can lead to greater things over time.
- It should show an understanding that the canyon is an example of something forming slowly over time.

Q11.
Give a score of 0, 1, or 2 based on how many relevant details from the caption are given.

- Possible answers include that the canyon took millions of years to form, that water wore the rock away a little at a time, or that the canyon is now thousands of feet deep.

Q12. Use the Narrative Writing Rubric at the end of the answer key to give an overall score out of 10.

Practice Set 17

Question	Answer	Indiana Academic Standard
1	B	Identify relationships among words, including synonyms, antonyms, homographs, homonyms, and multiple-meaning words (e.g., puzzle, fire).
2	B	Identify relationships among words, including synonyms, antonyms, homographs, homonyms, and multiple-meaning words (e.g., puzzle, fire).
3	B	Distinguish among the purposes of various media messages, including for information, entertainment, persuasion, interpretation of events, or transmission of culture.
4	A	Identify how a nonfiction text can be structured to indicate a problem and solution or to put events in chronological order.
5	C	Recognize the meanings of idioms in context.
6	A	Distinguish among the purposes of various media messages, including for information, entertainment, persuasion, interpretation of events, or transmission of culture.
7	See Below	Ask and answer questions to demonstrate understanding of a text, referring explicitly to the text as the basis for the answers.
8	See Below	Apply knowledge of text features to locate information and gain meaning from a text (e.g., maps, illustrations, charts, font/format).
9	D	Distinguish one's own perspective from that of the author of the text.
10	B	Ask and answer questions to demonstrate understanding of a text, referring explicitly to the text as the basis for the answers.
11	See Below	Distinguish between fact and opinion; explain how an author uses reasons and facts to support specific points in a text.
12	See Below	Distinguish between fact and opinion; explain how an author uses reasons and facts to support specific points in a text.

Q7.
Give a score of 0, 1, or 2 based on how many correct areas are given.
- The areas covered may include keeping fit and healthy, keeping active, reading and speaking, learning math, or learning English skills.

Q8.
Give a score of 0, 1, or 2 based on how well the answer meets the criteria listed below.
- It should identify the main purpose as being to describe some of the activities, to give examples of what the child will do, or to make the activities sound fun and/or useful.
- It should use relevant details from the passage.

Q11.
Give a score of 0, 1, or 2 based on how many acceptable reasons are given.
- Possible reasons listed could include that children under the age of five learn fitness habits they will keep for life, learn quickly, take in information quickly, and develop skills easier.

Q12.
Give a score of 0, 1, or 2 based on how well the answer meets the criteria listed below.
- It should describe at least three benefits to children of attending the Shining Light Day Center.
- The benefits described should be based on the information in the passage.
- It should use relevant details from the passage.

Practice Set 18

Question	Answer	Indiana Academic Standard
1	B	Describe characters in a story (e.g., their traits, motivations, or feelings) and explain how their actions contribute to the plot.
2	A	Ask and answer questions to demonstrate understanding of a text, referring explicitly to the text as the basis for the answers.
3	D	Use terms such as chapter, scene, and stanza to refer to the parts of stories, plays, and poems; describe how each successive part builds on earlier sections.
4	D	Explain how specific aspects of a text's illustrations contribute to what is conveyed by the words in a story.
5	See Below	Ask and answer questions to demonstrate understanding of a text, referring explicitly to the text as the basis for the answers.
6	See Below	Distinguish personal point of view from that of the narrator or those of the characters.
7	B	Describe characters in a story (e.g., their traits, motivations, or feelings) and explain how their actions contribute to the plot.
8	B	Ask and answer questions to demonstrate understanding of a text, referring explicitly to the text as the basis for the answers.
9	A	Ask and answer questions to demonstrate understanding of a text, referring explicitly to the text as the basis for the answers.
10	C	Explain how specific aspects of a text's illustrations contribute to what is conveyed by the words in a story.
11	See Below	Ask and answer questions to demonstrate understanding of a text, referring explicitly to the text as the basis for the answers.
12	See Below	Compare and contrast the themes, settings, and plots of stories written by the same author about the same or similar characters.

Q5.
Give a score of 0, 1, or 2 based on how well the answer meets the criteria listed below.
- It should explain that Max is staying home, whereas Quinn and Hoy are going away.

Q6.
Give a score of 0, 1, or 2 based on how well the answer meets the criteria listed below.
- It should give a personal opinion on whether the plans sound interesting or dull.
- It should explain why the student has that opinion.

Q11.
Give a score of 0, 1, or 2 based on how well the answer meets the criteria listed below.
- The table should be completed with reasonable inferences and relevant supporting details.
- Where the story takes place / at a lake / They find a good spot near the lake.
- What time of day the story takes place / around noon / It is warm and gets warmer.
- What time of year the story takes place / summer / It is a warm day.

Q12.
Give a score of 0, 1, or 2 based on how well the answer meets the criteria listed below.
- It should show how you can tell that Max and Sam both like to make the most out of things.
- It should refer to how Max is looking forward to his vacation at home and to how Sam suggests fishing with the candy worms.
- It should use relevant details from both passages.

Practice Set 19

Question	Answer	Indiana Academic Standard
1	See Below	Conduct short research on a topic. Locate information in reference texts, electronic resources, or through interviews.
2	See Below	Conduct short research on a topic. Record relevant information in their own words.
3	See Below	Write persuasive compositions in a variety of forms that state the opinion in an introductory statement or section.
4	See Below	Write persuasive compositions in a variety of forms that support the opinion with reasons in an organized way.
5	A Day of Learning	Edit writing for format and convention. Demonstrate command of capitalization, punctuation, and spelling.
6	C	Edit writing for format and convention. Demonstrate command of English grammar and usage.
7	B	Edit writing for format and convention. Demonstrate command of English grammar and usage.
8	A	Edit writing for format and convention. Demonstrate command of capitalization, punctuation, and spelling.
9	B	Edit writing for format and convention. Demonstrate command of English grammar and usage.
10	more	Edit writing for format and convention. Demonstrate command of capitalization, punctuation, and spelling.
11	bursts	Edit writing for format and convention. Demonstrate command of capitalization, punctuation, and spelling.
12	C	Edit writing for format and convention. Demonstrate command of English grammar and usage.
13	C	Edit writing for format and convention. Demonstrate command of English grammar and usage.
14	there	Edit writing for format and convention. Demonstrate command of capitalization, punctuation, and spelling.
15	D	Edit writing for format and convention. Demonstrate command of capitalization, punctuation, and spelling.
16	B	Edit writing for format and convention. Demonstrate command of English grammar and usage.
17	A	Edit writing for format and convention. Demonstrate command of capitalization, punctuation, and spelling.
18	saw	Edit writing for format and convention. Demonstrate command of capitalization, punctuation, and spelling.
19	D	Edit writing for format and convention. Demonstrate command of English grammar and usage.
20	A	Edit writing for format and convention. Demonstrate command of capitalization, punctuation, and spelling.
21	A	Edit writing for format and convention. Demonstrate command of English grammar and usage.
22	C	Edit writing for format and convention. Demonstrate command of capitalization, punctuation, and spelling.

Q1.
Give a score of 1 for each correct sentence circled. The following two sentences should be circled.
- At that time the land was not thought to be worth much.
- No one then had discovered the fact that beneath Penn's Woods there were huge amounts of coal and iron, which would one day be of greater value than all the riches of the king of England.

Q2.
Give a score of 0, 1, or 2 based on how well the answer meets the criteria listed below.
- It should explain how King Charles made an error when giving the land away so cheaply.
- The paragraph should use the supporting details circled.

Q3.
Give a score of 0, 1, or 2 based on how well the answer meets the criteria listed below.
- It should provide a reasonable opening that introduces the topic and states the main claim.
- The opening should be based on the claim that you should keep trying new things.

Q4.
Give a score of 0, 1, or 2 based on how well the answer meets the criteria listed below.
- The paragraph should make an argument about how people should keep trying new things.
- The argument made should be based on one of the supporting ideas listed.

Practice Set 20

Question	Answer	Indiana Academic Standard
1	A	Determine the meanings of general academic and content-specific words and phrases in a nonfiction text.
2	B	Identify how a nonfiction text can be structured to indicate a problem and solution or to put events in chronological order.
3	D	Determine the main idea of a text; recount the key details and explain how they support the main idea.
4	A	Apply knowledge of text features to locate information and gain meaning from a text (e.g., maps, illustrations, charts, font/format).
5	See Below	Ask and answer questions to demonstrate understanding of a text, referring explicitly to the text as the basis for the answers.
6	See Below	Describe the relationship between a series of historical events, scientific ideas or concepts, or steps in processes or procedures in a text, using words such as first, next, finally, because, problem, solution, same, and different.
7	B	Apply context clues (e.g., word, phrase, and sentence clues) and text features (e.g., maps, illustrations, charts) to determine the meanings of unknown words.
8	B	Determine the main idea of a text; recount the key details and explain how they support the main idea.
9	B	Distinguish between fact and opinion; explain how an author uses reasons and facts to support specific points in a text.
10	See Below	Distinguish between fact and opinion; explain how an author uses reasons and facts to support specific points in a text.
11	See Below	Ask and answer questions to demonstrate understanding of a text, referring explicitly to the text as the basis for the answers.
12	See Below	Write informative compositions on a variety of topics.

Q5.
Give a score of 0, 1, or 2 based on how well the answer meets the criteria listed below.
- The web should be completed with three early businesses of Nintendo.
- The early businesses are maker of playing cards, taxi company, television network, and food company.

Q6.
Give a score of 0, 1, or 2 based on how well the answer meets the criteria listed below.
- It should list the entertainment products released by Nintendo in order from earliest to most recent.
- The products released in order from earliest to latest are: Nintendo Entertainment System (1983); Game Boy (1989); Nintendo DS (2004); and Nintendo Wii (2006).

Q10.
Give a score of 0, 1, or 2 based on how many correct comparisons are given.
- The answer may describe how other computers had their parts in a separate case while the iMac G3 had its parts in the monitor, how other computers were drab colors while the iMac G3 was bright, how the style of the iMac G3 was liked more, or how the iMac G3 took up less space.

Q11.
Give a score of 0, 1, or 2 based on how well the answer meets the criteria listed below.
- It should describe how Steve Jobs created a product that people would like when he made the iMac G3.
- It should use relevant details from the passage and the caption to show that the product was liked.

Q12. Use the Informative Writing Rubric at the end of the answer key to give an overall score out of 10.

Practice Set 21

Use the Opinion Writing Rubric at the end of the answer key to give an overall score out of 10.

Practice Set 22

Use the Informative Writing Rubric at the end of the answer key to give an overall score out of 10.

OPINION WRITING RUBRIC

This writing rubric is based on the state standards and is the same criteria used to assess writing tasks on the ILEARN tests. Give students an overall score out of 4 for Organization/Purpose and for Evidence/Elaboration. Give students a score out of 2 for Conventions. Combine the scores for a total out of 10. Students can also be given feedback and guidance based on the criteria below.

	Score	Notes
Organization/Purpose To receive a full score, the response will have the features listed below. • opinion is introduced, clearly communicated, and the focus is strongly maintained for the purpose and audience • consistent use of a variety of transitional strategies to clarify the relationships between and among ideas • effective introduction and conclusion • logical progression of ideas from beginning to end; strong connections between and among ideas with some syntactic variety	/4	
Evidence/Elaboration To receive a full score, the response will have the features listed below. • comprehensive evidence (facts and details) from the source material is integrated, relevant, and specific • clear citations or attribution of source material • effective use of a variety of elaborative techniques • vocabulary is clearly appropriate for the audience and purpose • effective, appropriate style enhances content	/4	
Conventions To receive a full score, the response will: • have adequate use of correct sentence formation, punctuation, capitalization, grammar usage, and spelling	/2	
Total Score	/10	

INFORMATIVE WRITING RUBRIC

This writing rubric is based on the state standards and is the same criteria used to assess writing tasks on the ILEARN tests. Give students an overall score out of 4 for Organization/Purpose and for Evidence/Elaboration. Give students a score out of 2 for Conventions. Combine the scores for a total out of 10. Students can also be given feedback and guidance based on the criteria below.

	Score	Notes
Organization/Purpose To receive a full score, the response will have the features listed below. • controlling/main idea of a topic is clearly communicated, and the focus is strongly maintained for the purpose and audience • consistent use of a variety of transitional strategies to clarify the relationships between and among ideas • effective introduction and conclusion • logical progression of ideas from beginning to end; strong connections between and among ideas with some syntactic variety	/4	
Evidence/Elaboration To receive a full score, the response will have the features listed below. • comprehensive evidence (facts and details) from the source material is integrated, relevant, and specific • clear citations or attribution of source material • effective use of a variety of elaborative techniques • vocabulary is clearly appropriate for the audience and purpose • effective, appropriate style enhances content	/4	
Conventions To receive a full score, the response will: • have adequate use of correct sentence formation, punctuation, capitalization, grammar usage, and spelling	/2	
Total Score	/10	

NARRATIVE WRITING RUBRIC

This writing rubric is based on the state standards and is the same criteria used to assess writing tasks on the ILEARN tests. Give students an overall score out of 4 for Organization/Purpose and for Development/Elaboration. Give students a score out of 2 for Conventions. Combine the scores for a total out of 10. Students can also be given feedback and guidance based on the criteria below.

	Score	Notes
Organization/Purpose To receive a full score, the response will have the features listed below. • an effective plot helps to create a sense of unity and completeness • effectively establishes a setting, narrator/characters, and/or point of view • consistent use of a variety of transitional strategies to clarify the relationships between and among ideas; strong connection between and among ideas • natural, logical sequence of events • effective opening and closure for audience and purpose	/4	
Development/Elaboration To receive a full score, the response will have the features listed below. • experiences, characters, setting and/or events are clearly developed • effective use of a variety of narrative techniques that advance the story or illustrate the experience • effective use of sensory, concrete, and figurative language that clearly advances the purpose • effective, appropriate style enhances the narration	/4	
Conventions To receive a full score, the response will: • have adequate use of correct sentence formation, punctuation, capitalization, grammar usage, and spelling	/2	
Total Score	/10	

Made in the USA
Monee, IL
29 February 2020

22402448R00116